Hear Me Out

Hear Me Out

SARAH HARDING

WITH TERRY RONALD

EBURY
PRESS

1 3 5 7 9 10 8 6 4 2

Ebury Press, an imprint of Ebury Publishing
20 Vauxhall Bridge Road
London SW1V 2SA

Ebury Press is part of the Penguin Random House group of companies
whose addresses can be found at global.penguinrandomhouse.com

Penguin
Random House
UK

Copyright © Sarah Harding 2021

Sarah Harding has asserted her right to be identified as the author of this Work
in accordance with the Copyright, Designs and Patents Act 1988

First published by Ebury Press in 2021
This paperback edition published in 2022

www.penguin.co.uk

A CIP catalogue record for this book is available from the British Library

ISBN 9781529109764

The publisher and author have made every effort to credit the copyright
owners of any material that appears within, and will correct any
omissions in subsequent editions if notified.

Permissions and Picture Credits

Section 1: p. 1 and p. 2 © Shutterstock; p. 3 top left © Sarah Harding,
top right © Polydor, below left © Shutterstock and below right © Sarah Harding;
p. 4 © Sarah Harding; p. 5 ©Polydor; p. 6 ©Polydor, except top left © Getty
Images; p. 7 © Polydor' except middle left © Getty Images; p. 8 © Sarah
Harding, below middle © FameFlyNet and row 4 far left © Shutterstock

Section 2: p. 1 © Shutterstock; p. 2 top right © Peter Loraine, middle
© Sarah Harding, middle © Camera Press, below © Terry Ronald, right
© Getty Images; p. 3 © with kind permission of Sarah Harding fans;
p. 4 top © Sarah Harding, below left © Channel 4, below right Shutterstock;
p. 5 top © Shutterstock, below Getty Images; p. 6 © Shutterstock; p. 7 top
© Getty Images, middle © Sarah Harding, below © Shutterstock;
Page 8 © Sarah Harding End pages: © Elisabeth Hoff

Printed and bound in Great Britain by Clays Ltd, Elcograf S.p.A.
The authorised representative in the EEA is Penguin Random House Ireland,
Morrison Chambers, 32 Nassau Street, Dublin D02 YH68

MIX
Paper from
responsible sources
FSC
www.fsc.org   FSC® C018179

Penguin Random House is committed to a
sustainable future for our business, our readers
and our planet. This book is made from Forest
Stewardship Council® certified paper.

For my mum.

Thank you for all your support and love.

And for putting up with me.

Love you x

CONTENTS

PROLOGUE

t's strange, this world I find myself in. It's like I've stepped on to another planet where everything seems unfamiliar. I suppose everybody could say that in the midst of a global pandemic, but that's not it for me. As I write this, it's a few weeks before my 39th birthday, and I have no idea what's waiting for me in the year to come. Nothing is certain any more.

As most of you will know, I have cancer. Cancer that has spread from its original site in my breast to my lung, making it much harder to treat. I'm doing my absolute best to be positive and to fight it. Still, it seems that, even with the best immunotherapy, I'll be looking at two years maximum.

As those of you who have been through something like this know, some days are easier than others. During my ongoing chemotherapy treatment, I have good days and bad days.

On the good ones I find myself getting a bit restless, not knowing what to do with myself. I have a busy mind and always have had; that's one of the reasons I decided to write this book. It's given me something positive to focus on. It's also a chance to reflect on everything, good and bad, and to remind myself what a wonderfully full and colourful life I've had up to this point. A life I'm very grateful for, having achieved above and beyond anything I dreamed of when I was a little girl.

The other reason for writing my book now is that it's, I suppose, a way to set a few things straight. Everyone has an opinion, that's a given, and I imagine most people picking up my book will have an opinion about me – some good; some maybe not so good. We all make judgements about people we think we know; it's human nature. I can't rewrite history; all I can do is be as honest as I can and wear my heart on my sleeve. That's something that hasn't always worked out for me in the past, but it's really the only way I know.

I've done my best to be honest and get it all down, although it's probably better that I don't tell you absolutely everything now – otherwise, there'll be nothing left to put in a sequel!

One of the things I'd like to achieve with my book is to show people the real me. Or perhaps remind them. I suppose that's one of the reasons many people write an autobiography, but for me it's especially relevant. When I look back at my time in Girls Aloud, I feel like I became a caricature. OK, so maybe I put out a particular image, which the press and media latched on to. It was an easy one to work with: rock chick, blonde bombshell, party girl, the caner of the band. For me, it was like, 'Oh! That's who I am then. I've been looking for my role in the band, so this must be it.' So, in that respect I suppose it became easy for me as well. Convenient. I mean, I liked a drink, I was a bit rebellious, I liked to go out partying, so it was a win/win. Until it wasn't.

Somewhere among the nightclubs, the frocks and hairdos, the big chart hits and the glamour of being a pop star, the other Sarah Harding got utterly lost. I'm saying the *other* Sarah rather than the *real* Sarah because there is most definitely that fun, crazy party girl in me – there always was. It was the other Sarah – the one who liked curling up at home with her dog and a good book; the one who enjoyed cooking a roast dinner for her friends; the one who liked spending nights alone, writing songs and making music – who got lost. She's the one who's been forgotten. Yet she's still here. She's right here talking to you now. And all she wants is for you to hear her out. Now more than ever: hear me out.

CHAPTER ONE

What do little girls dream of becoming? Princesses? Politicians? Athletes or astronauts? Nurses or mothers? All of the above, I suppose, depending on the little girl. Well, my dream was crystal clear from the start. I wanted to be a pop star. Wait, that's not exactly true. Not a pop star – a singer. I wanted to sing, and I wanted people to hear me sing. I wanted to perform and to have everyone watch me. At family gatherings, when I was little, I gave performances for my parents and anyone else I could get to watch.

'Now sit down, everyone,' I'd say, 'I'm about to sing.'

Only it wasn't that simple. It wasn't just that I wanted to sing for people – I also wanted to get some kind of reaction to what I was doing; for people to think I was good at it. I wanted to be loved and accepted.

I suppose that's all I've ever really wanted.

As I got older, music and singing continued to dominate my childhood dreams. My dad, John, was hugely into music. A talented musician in his own right, he played lead guitar, piano and bass, and he sang too. I vividly remember the photograph of him and his guitar, which was on display at my gran-ny's house. Dad has been in quite a few bands over the years, and one of the things we have in common is that we've both performed at *The Royal Variety Performance* and met the Queen. How cool is that?

I was never what you'd call a girly girl, even back then. That said, I enjoyed art and drawing very much. One of my early efforts was a picture of myself being filmed by a camera crew walking towards a front door. Maybe it was my very own little prediction of what was to come; I don't know. I always loved cooking, too, right from when I was a little girl, and I remember being in the Brownies, making a mean sausage and mash, which is still one of my favourites. Maybe it's because my mum has always made the best mashed potato – I guess it's the Irish in us.

Whatever the time of day, if I had my eyes open, I was always active. Always busy doing something. If I wasn't playing the piano in the house, I was out in the garden in the mud, trying to find frogs or climbing trees. I always like the option of being able to run away and hide somewhere, to escape. I found myself a little hideaway up a tree at the bottom of the garden; my fortress, I called it. Whenever I was in trouble or Mum or Dad came after me, or if I wanted to be on my own, I'd run to my fortress, high in the tree. It wasn't an especially complicated structure, but it did have a pulley system, which I'd made myself.

'Mum, can I have a sandwich, please?' I'd shout.

Mum would put the sandwich on the pulley, and I'd bring it all the way up to the top of the tree. My fortress was also great for pranks. Sometimes, when we had friends round, us kids would be up in the fortress dropping water bombs on people, like the little shits we were.

What I loved most of all was playing Dad's guitars. He would re-string them every weekend and let me strum away. I even got my own guitar eventually; a pale-pink Marlin Sidewinder, and, to go with it, a mini Marshall amp. There was nothing I loved more than plugging my little pink guitar in and playing in the corner of the room.

Quite often, you could find me standing in front of the hi-fi, singing along to Mariah Carey or Whitney Houston, just waiting for my dad to come home from the rehearsal studio so I could show my voice off to him. I loved singing along to those big divas, trying to reach the notes that they could. Even then, I felt like I was getting my voice strong, ready for when I became a professional singer.

I guess my upbringing was what you might call unconventional. My mum, dad and I lived in a village called Wraysbury, which is in the Royal Borough of Windsor and Maidenhead, and directly under the approach path of Heathrow airport. I have a half-brother, Dave, who is sixteen years older than me – Mum's son from a previous marriage. Back then we didn't really get on with one another, probably because of the huge age gap. He was a member of The Monster Raving Loony Party, which was, and still is, a bizarre satirical political party started by a guy called David Sutch, AKA Screaming Lord Sutch. My brother's title was Sir Dangerous, and I remember seeing a recording of him from back in the day: Dave and Lord Sutch on cable TV, interviewed by none other than Sacha Baron Cohen.

Another peculiar thing about my childhood was the number of schools I attended. Rather than two, or maybe three schools, like most kids, I went to seven. I know, seven! I wish I could tell you why I went to so many schools, but the truth is I don't know, not really. What I do know is that I was not an easy child to manage, mainly because from a young age I had ADHD – attention deficit hyperactivity disorder. It's a condition that affects people's behaviour, making them appear restless and impulsive. People with ADHD can have trouble concentrating or display signs of manic behaviour, depending on the severity of the individual case. It started when I was tiny, and it would be something I'd have to learn to live with always.

While I was at kindergarten, and at the start of infants' school, I used to go to see a woman, a child psychologist, who would regularly assess me. At the same time, I played with all the toys in her office. While I invented games, playing happily, she would talk to me and take notes, asking me questions about the games and what was happening in my created world.

Of course, I had no idea why this was happening back then; I assume it was some kind of play therapy to find out what made me tick. I guess my parents needed to find out why I had a seemingly endless amount of energy, which was very much the case; I mean, I was hardly ever sitting down quietly. Usually, I was running around, breaking things or cutting off my doll's hair. I remember having two Barbies but desperately wanting a Ken so I could marry one of them off. Mum wouldn't buy me a Ken, so I cut off one of the Barbie's hair in an attempt to turn her into a bloke. Essentially, at the age of five, I had lesbian Barbies, who were married by the taps of the bath while I was in the tub with an entire kingdom of toys. Eventually, the child psychologist arrived at the ADHD diagnosis. Still, I wasn't given medication at first because everyone felt I was too young. I didn't start taking medication until years later when I was in the band and struggling somewhat with the pressures of fame.

So back to the seven schools. I suppose I was feeling a different kind of pressure then; the pressure of constantly adapting to new environments.

I was about nine when my parents sent me to a boarding school called Thornton College in Buckinghamshire. The school had daily students and weekly borders. I was a termly border, meaning I only went home during school holidays. While I was boarding, my mum went to Manchester to do a counsel-ling course at Manchester University. Being a music teacher and a working musician, my dad's schedule was all over the place, so they thought boarding school was the answer. The college wasn't that far from where we lived in Buckinghamshire, so, as a child, it was hard for me to grasp why I couldn't go home more often. It's something I touched on in therapy later on in life, and something I've asked my parents about too. What was going on in their marriage that they couldn't have me there all the time? I guess I didn't realise how hard things were for them back then. My mum really missed her family up north and wanted to better herself, and my dad was working all the hours God sent to make money.

Thornton was an ancient building and run by nuns. I wouldn't say I liked it at all. There was a cavernous room with pillars called the Red Hall, which could be very scary, especially at night when you had to walk across it and couldn't find the light switch. It was called The Red Hall because a nun had apparently once hung herself from the top of the stairs and blood had dripped down on to the floor. Like most kids, I believed in all the ghost stories I heard, so I was always terrified if I had to cross the musty, cobweb-filled Red Hall on my own. I'd run from one pillar to the other, convinced the ghost of the dead nun would get me.

The good things I remember about the place is having piano and music lessons, which was something to look forward to each week. Also, the fact that there were lots of Spanish girls at the college, which meant I picked up a lot of the language.

Our matron was in her late thirties and looked exactly like Miss Hannigan from *Annie*, with short hair and a gap in her teeth. I'm not sure why, but she took a dislike to me and also another little girl from Zimbabwe, Rudo, who was the youngest in the school. I was the second youngest. I never knew why, she just wasn't very nice to us, which made my experience pretty miserable.

We slept in dorms where we also played marathon card games at weekends, and we all ate in one big hall. Some nights, Rudo and I would steal out of bed so we could go and chat with the other girls. A few times we got caught, and Matron would make us stand in the corridor, facing the wall for hours. It was pretty brutal.

I wasn't aware of it at the time, but I'd only got into the school because I'd passed several tests and been awarded a bursary. The school fees were expensive, and my parents would never have been able to afford to send me there had I not been bright. God, if I'd known that, I would have played dumb, flunked the bloody exams and gone to a regular school.

My half-brother Dave was the only one who ever visited me at Thornton. He turned out to be a bit of a hero, and in more ways than one.

It all started when he came to one of the school's disco nights, which I ended up getting kicked out of. I know, can you imagine? Nine years old and thrown out of my first disco! What could possibly have been the reason, you might ask. Well, I'd recently seen the movie *Dirty Dancing*. I thought it would be a rather excellent idea to try out some of the provocative, grinding moves I'd learned from the film, at a disco full of pre-teen girls. The nuns weren't happy, despite my brother explaining that I was only a kid copying what I'd seen in the movie.

'No, it's not on,' Matron had said. 'Get her out!'

I was unceremoniously hauled away, while Dave went on to try to reason with her. In the end, she invited him 'for coffee' that evening and, strangely enough, after that night, she was a lot less horrible. In fact, she never said a bad word to me and was sometimes even nice. I didn't know it at the time, but it seems my

15

brother's coffee may have turned into something more than just coffee. It's possible he'd taken one for the team!

Despite the change in Matron's attitude, I still wasn't happy. I was constantly homesick and missed my parents. All in all, I was at Thornton for a year, and it was a lonely, tough year. During my time there, I began to have panic attacks and stopped eating properly because I was so anxious all the time, so I was thrilled to be out of there. Still, there was more unhappiness to come.

I was offered a place at a prep school called St Mary's, but Mum and Dad found out that the deputy head of Thornton was taking over as head at a school called Godstowe, where I could also board. I think my parents thought that my ex-deputy head might show me some favour and look after me, but it didn't really work out like that. I remember my dad driving me to Godstowe, trying to be terribly enthusiastic. He and his brothers had gone to boarding school, which Dad seemingly loved and hated in equal measure. Dad's father had been a doctor in the RAF during the Second World War and a practising GP after that. His mum – my granny – was a quite middle-class lady who played the piano beautifully.

'You're going to love it,' he'd told me as we'd driven towards the gates. 'It'll be just like St Trinian's.'

I wasn't quite ten years old and had no idea what St Trinian's was. Years later, of course, the irony was that I ended up in the part of Roxy in the movie, *St Trinian's: The Legend of Fritton's Gold*. The St Trinian's films go back years. They're centred around a boarding school for girls where the pupils are all juvenile delinquents:

smoking, gambling and getting up to all sorts of crazy mischief. I don't know; maybe if my school had been a bit more like St Trinian's, I'd have enjoyed it more.

Godstowe was much closer to home. True, I was still boarding, but at least I got to come home on exeat weekends. Again, I didn't really settle. The school was full of middle-class girls, lots of whom came from families with money. I came from a working-class background, and once again I'd got into the school purely on my grades. The trouble was, I wasn't all that interested in the more academic subjects. Instead, I lived for sports, music and drama. I loved netball and basketball and horses, and I was mad about singing and the idea of acting. That was the good thing about Godstowe; I could play sports and indulge my passion for all things musical.

On the downside, it was at Godstowe where I developed a phobia that stayed with me for years. Emetophobia is a fear of vomit, and in my case it was a fear of seeing another person throwing up. It started when there was a horrible stomach bug going around the school. It spread like wildfire around the dorm, and, in the middle of one night, the girl in the top bunk above me threw up violently. You can just imagine the sound of her retching and the sick hitting the floor. For weeks afterwards, I slept with my hands over my ears in case it happened again. In the end, I caught the bug, too; everyone did. There was constant sickness and vomiting all around me – it was torture. It got so bad that I couldn't go to sleep without being curled up with my fingers in my ears, even when I was at home – just in case I heard someone throwing up.

These days, the phobia isn't so bad, although I'm still not great around someone who's ill or being sick. Still, there have been times when I've even been able to hold a friend's hair back while her head is stuck in a toilet bowl after having one too many cocktails. I have to say, this is usually when I've been twatted myself, so possibly slightly numb to the situation. Mostly, I keep a safe distance away, giving the customary bang on the toilet door and shouting, 'Are you all right in there, babes? Do you need anything?' while they chuck their guts up.

After a year at Godstowe, not settling down, I went back to my old state primary school for the final year. It was so weird being back with some of the kids I'd been with when I was little. I'd been away from them for two years, and suddenly I had to get used to a whole new routine and way of life all over again. It wasn't the first time it had happened, and it certainly wasn't to be the last.

CHAPTER TWO

As I write this, I'm back in the family home again. Throughout my cancer treatment, I've been living with my mum, Marié. Thank God for her, and the small team of friends that I trust. I don't know how I'd have got through the last few months without Mum, and my friends Anna and Mousey. The truth is I wouldn't have.

At some points in our lives, Mum and I weren't as close as we should have been. Although it's really not the case, she can sometimes come across a bit shy and mild on first meeting. Over the years, that has led to certain people taking advantage of her. Being protective of her, it made me upset and angry, and I think I somehow resented her for letting it happen. It put a bit of distance between us for a while. As well as that, I always felt like I had to be independent. I learned it from an early age, being away from home at boarding school. Even though there were other kids and teachers around, I was out in the world on my own, away from home and family. You don't have any choice but to learn how to survive on your own.

Mum is in her late seventies now, and she has become everything to me through this illness, especially since I've been staying with her. I know how hard this is on her too. I often worry about her, especially as she's gotten older. I can't bear the thought of anything happening to her. In a strange way it's comforting to know that I will probably leave this world before she does; at least then I won't have to go through the pain of losing her. The truth is, I can't live without her now. She cares for me and helps me because, at times, I am too weak to help myself.

Luckily, Mum is really healthy; in fact, she doesn't stop. For the last couple of days, for instance, I've felt exhausted, so Mum has done all the cooking. She just gets on with it. She's been strong because she has to be. I guess now we're closer than ever.

Mum's house is in the middle of nowhere. There's not really much to do, so on a day like today, when I'm feeling up to it, I've been reorganising my room here. What I'm really hoping is that I'm going to be able to have my own place again soon. I've had my eye on an apartment that's not far from Mum's, and I've asked my lawyer friend – Tricia, who helps looks after my affairs – to find out if there's a chance I might be able to rent it. Of course, there are all sorts of concerns about me striking out on my own, particularly with my current health issues. Still, I'm pretty confident that, with help, and my mum being nearby, I can do it.

Having my own space is vital to me; it always has been. While people might rightly think of me as a social animal, there's a big part of me that craves quiet and privacy. It's the yin and yang in me.

Until then, I've made a nice little space for myself here at Mum's place. My bedroom is a little haven with some soft twinkly lights over the bed, and my computer to hand if I get the urge to put some track ideas together. My love of music is the thing that has always kept me going, and over the years I've taught myself to use technology to put my new tracks together. It started off with DJ decks and a mixer. I enjoyed playing a few gigs and dropping tunes at home for my mates while we shared a few bottles of vino, but I eventually realised I wasn't cut out to be a superstar DJ. That was when I progressed to music software, where I could create my own sounds and music.

Whether or not anyone hears what I've created is not all that important. It's the creative process that means something to me; making something from nothing and hearing it come to life. When I'm focused, on my own, I can sit up half the night mucking about with sounds and beats. I get lost in it; although you'll understand when I tell you that it hasn't been all that easy lately.

When you have cancer, it takes over everything, and I don't mean just the disease. I mean the treatment, the appointments, the mountains of medication, the strict timetable of everything, the rules about what you can and can't do and where you should or shouldn't go. While the rest of the world is going on around you, it's like living on your own little planet. When you add to that the weirdness of 2020, with Covid-19 and the lockdown, and then straight into another lockdown at the start of 2021, my whole world just feels surreal at the moment. It's why writing this book is so important. It's something for me to focus on, something positive.

Like most kids back in the day, I loved to go out and play. Right from the off, I was a tomboy. I was that kid who was always knocking on the neighbourhood doors.

'Can so-and-so come out to play?'

Back then, I hung out with more boys than I did girls. I loved being out on my bike, and you wouldn't catch me dead in a dress. My fashion was cut-off trousers or snazzy leggings – I fondly remember a little spotty pair I had. Of course, there were always jeans, and because of the era – late eighties, early nineties – there was the inevitable shell suit. God, when I think back, it's hard to imagine ever wearing one of those things, but back then I was obsessed. I remember having a blue one with little bits of yellow and pink on. Absolutely hideous, but at the time I loved it.

There was a cricket green near us, so sometimes I'd play cricket with the boys, or we could be found in the local park, climbing trees, which was always a massive thrill. Some of the trees in our local park were old and huge, and it was always a competition to see who could get the highest the fastest. There was one enormous tree that was the biggest challenge. Once you got up to the lowest branch, you'd have to swing like Mowgli, throwing your legs upwards to wrap around the branch, which was just a little higher up. Higher and higher we'd go, never worrying about how the hell we were going to get down again.

My daredevil antics didn't stop at climbing trees, however. When I was about ten or eleven years old, I decided that I was going to run away from home. I can't remember what prompted me to do it at the time that I did, but I remember that, for some reason, I'd been banished to my bedroom and I was not happy. I knew if I was to achieve any kind of successful escape, I certainly wasn't going to be able to stroll down the stairs and out of the front door. Instead, I decided that my bedroom window was the best option. Unfortunately, my bedroom was on the first floor, much too high to jump from, so I was going to have to come up with a plan.

I figured that if I fashioned some kind of rope, I could throw it out of the window and slide down it; surely it couldn't be much different to climbing up or down a rope in a PE lesson, right? I gathered together what looked like my most sturdy tops and jumpers and started tying them together. Once I had what looked like a long enough rope, I tied one end of it to my bed and threw the other bit out of the window, almost to the ground.

Determined to make a clean getaway, I clambered out the window. I started shimmying down the stretchy, woolly rope, but the further I got, the looser the knots in the jumper appeared to be getting. At one point, Mum and Dad, who were watching TV at the time, looked out of the living room window only to witness their pre-teen daughter swinging precariously on a rope that was literally coming apart at the seams. Mum told me that they actually only got a brief glimpse of me dangling there before they heard a massive thud and I shot past their line of sight. Not unexpectedly, the jumpers had loosened and come apart, and I'd gone flying towards the ground below. Luckily, I wasn't too badly hurt, but I certainly gave Mum and Dad a scare. I can't really remember if my plans to run away went any further or whether I just gave up after that.

It was around that time when I became friends with Gena; I called her my cousin although we weren't actually related. Our mums were very friendly, and I used to call her mum Auntie Julie, hence everyone thinking that Gena and I were cousins. The two of us loved horses, so we'd often go down to the nearby stables and fields where we could take horses out to ride. I never owned a horse, there was no way our family could have afforded that. Instead, I'd found a card in a newsagents window after school one day advertising the loaning of a pony called Jago.

Jago belonged to a girl called Deanie, who'd grown out of him and had got a bigger horse. Her family bred horses for show jumping and were a lovely and down-to-earth bunch. As it was just down the road from us, I thought this would be the perfect way for me to be able to ride regularly. Before that, I'd gone to Kate Hamilton's stables, which was a trek all the way to Virginia Water. There I had to help out, cleaning and mucking out the stables as a way to subsidise my lessons. With this new set-up, Deanie gave lessons for a fiver an hour, much closer to home. I started smaller on a pony called Pandora, who was a 13.2-hands pony, but then moved on to Jago. A 14.2 bay thoroughbred, she wasn't an easy horse by any means.

During the times when I wasn't boarding, I would get up at 6am every morning before school. I'd go down to Deanie's family stables, feed Jago, muck her out and take her out to the field to exercise her. (Side note, I'd always be getting late marks at school because of this.) Once school was over, I'd be back at the stables, riding or jumping her or going out on hacks with Gena.

Sometimes, Gena and I would be daring and ride bareback on the horses. Either we'd have a halter (headcollar) on the horse and ride cowboy-style, or we'd jump on the horse bareback: no stirrups, no saddle and no bridle. We'd race like cowboys without riding hats. I was only about 12 or 13 and this was the fearlessness and rebellion that came with youth, I suppose. Still, it was so dangerous. By some miracle, neither of us were ever hurt. Being on a horse, galloping through a field, was simply the most liberating feeling.

When I think of myself then, I remember feeling like such an ugly duckling. I had a grim little perm, just coming out of a goth phase, so I was continually spraying my hair with Sun In because I was so desperate to be blonde. I wasn't all that happy with myself. The horse riding made me happy, though, and kept me out of trouble, at least for a while.

After jumping from school to school in my primary years, I was expecting things to feel more settled when I started secondary school. At Salesians School, some of the kids thought of me as a bit of a geek because I was always in the music room. I was also still very much into sports, and it was here that I got into basketball, as well as participating in netball tournaments. I was also good at swimming, ice skating, athletics and liked running.

Nothing more than 100 metres, mind you; short distances were always the way to go as far as I was concerned. Anything longer than that, like cross-country, and I could be found sitting in the woods with my friend, puffing on a cigarette. We'd end up walking around the course chatting, rather than running.

My first proper boyfriend, Jayden, came on the scene when I was about fourteen or fifteen. We first met at a swimming pool disco, which is like a pool party, with everyone in the pool plunging down the slides with the wave machines going, while a mobile DJ plays loud music. Jayden lived on the Dedworth army estate, which, at the time, was quite rough and ready. I liked the idea of a bad boy, and he seemed like a bit of a tough cookie, which appealed. I guess some things never change. In fact, I have to admit, sometimes we didn't even make it into pool discos. Instead, we'd all end up hanging out in Windsor and wait until we found somebody who would kindly go into a shop and buy us some cider.

I guess it was always more fun for me to be in the naughty crowd; smoking behind the school shed and getting up to mischief. I'd been bullied a little, so hanging with a particular group of kids who were seen as a bit tougher was a way of protecting myself from being bullied. At least that's the way I saw it. There were groups of girls higher up in the school than me who I looked up to as big sisters; it was a safety thing.

Still, even within these groups, there were always plenty of dramas unfolding. I've got vivid memories of girls rowing in the toilets, and it was always the same old thing: 'she said this, and you said that and I heard you told so-and-so this, that or the other'. It was a bit rough and ready, my secondary school, but I loved it.

I was such a tomboy that I think sometimes the boys thought of me as one of them. I certainly had a fair amount of banter with the lads, and I enjoyed that. There were times, though, that I wanted to be the pretty blonde girl who walked home from school with a boy and got a snog along the way. I remember one girl who always kissed her boyfriend at the end of the alley that we had to walk down on the way back from school. I watched her being kissed, and I was always envious. I wanted that too, but in my heart I never believed that I was the right sort of girl to get that kind of attention from boys. I'd been a sweet blonde with ringlets when I was little, but now I had brown hair, which I thought of as drab. In fact, as far as I was concerned, my whole look was a bit 'meh'!

That's probably why I was able to have such banter with the boys without getting into too much grief. Other girls just didn't see me as a threat. That banter with guys is something I've carried throughout my life. I seem to have a knack of making men laugh, perhaps because I say stuff that they don't expect a woman to say. The difference now I'm grown-up is that, because of the way I look, I've sometimes been seen as a threat by some women. For this reason, I often have to be more careful about which men I'm having the banter with.

At Salesians, some of the teachers called me 'the catalyst'; it almost became a nick-name. As far as they were concerned, when-ever trouble or mischief was going on, I would be found right in the midst of it. I didn't deliberately set out to cause trouble, but I was undoubtedly the joker in the pack among my classmates. Laughing and joking around, not paying attention and generally being disruptive. Along with a couple of other girls in my group, I always seemed to be getting into grief with the teachers. Still, at the same time, we generally got top grades and were in the highest streams for most subjects. I don't know, perhaps that's why I thought I could get away with it. Eventually something had to give, and my luck was going to run out.

It got to the stage where my behaviour was having a negative effect on the other pupils, often dictating the way the lesson was going to go. In the end, it was decided by the powers that be that something drastic had to be done.

Once again, I was on the move. Yes, my parents sent me to yet another school, but this time the emphasis was on discipline: I was sent to military school. And yes, it was another bloody boarding school. I was thirteen years old when I entered Gordon's. By then, I was getting more interested in boys, and not just the banter, so I was relieved to find that this was at least a mixed-sex school.

It was here I decided that I wanted to become more of a girl's girl; ironic, I suppose, against the challenging backdrop of military school, but I remember it being a conscious decision: I wanted to have a boyfriend. I got my hair permed so I'd look more feminine, and did my best to try to be more girly. This was alongside wearing a CCF (Combined Cadet Force) uniform most of the time, and playing rugby in the rain and getting covered in mud most weekends. I was a proper GI Jane.

The regime there was pretty strict. Once a week we had to bull up our shoes until we could see our faces in them before taking them to show the sergeant. If we were ever caught coming in late, we were gated and made to run around the field at 6am with a hockey stick above our heads. It was hardcore, but on the upside, I did get to go home a lot more than I had at my previous boarding schools.

It was also here that I met a boy called Jake, who I used to go for a sneaky kiss with behind the rec. Once we'd finished our homework, we were allowed outside to mingle between houses, so it was the perfect opportunity for a quick bit of snogging. The trouble was, I was horribly shy. In fact, I could hardly look at Jake, despite thinking of him as my boyfriend. I felt very uncoordinated, and I was very self-conscious about my looks. I wanted to be that blonde, pretty girl that guys like but that girls liked too, but back then I didn't feel I was that. For this reason, I'd only agree to see Jake when it was dark so I didn't feel so exposed. This meant that we had to be quick with any snogging we did, as there was an 8pm cut-off point as far as mingling went, so you couldn't hang around.

At military school, I did shooting, assault courses, and took part in horse parades, but once again, it was fairly short-lived. I just couldn't cope with the strict discipline. I lasted six months before I was back at my old secondary school, Salesians, all ready for Year 9 into 10.

Unbelievably, that still wasn't it. It was options year, and I was still getting excellent grades, but that's right when Mum and Dad decided to move to Manchester. My mum's family were there, and she felt like she wanted to be closer to them. Looking back, I think that's when Mum and Dad's relationship started to flounder. It put a strain on their marriage. Dad's work as a musician was mostly based down south, so he ended up being away from home a lot. That certainly didn't help matters.

I remember preparing for the move, feeling miserable. I went into my room and started packing all my belongings into boxes: my CDs, my clothes, all my bits and pieces. This wasn't going to be easy, and I knew it.

One of the reasons it was so tough on me was because I'd only just started my GCSE options, and in my new local school the classes I wanted to take didn't have room for me. I guess I just lost interest after that and ended being stuck in the lower sets for every subject. By then, I was so fed up with being dragged out of different schools and the constant change that I just gave up. I know I wasn't always the easiest kid, particularly with my condition, which I wasn't on any medication for then; sometimes I felt like people didn't take that into consideration when dealing with me.

Being insecure meant that I'd pile on the make-up for school, but that, of course, was against the rules. I was always either in detention for wearing too much slap, or getting sent home to wash it off. My poor mum just didn't know what to do with me.

During my time at that final school, Dad was commuting down south for work, and Mum seemed to have lost all control over me. I was wagging off school, uninterested in the lessons because I was stuck in the bottom sets, not really being stimulated. I still played a bit of basketball, but I missed working with and riding horses, which I'd done throughout my time at the other schools.

The worst part about moving is that not long after we left, my gran, Dad's mum, was diagnosed with cancer, which took her quite quickly. The speed of it came as a complete shock. I knew she was very ill, but I just wasn't prepared to lose her that quickly. Luckily, my dad was able to be with her a lot of the time, but I didn't really get to see her. After she died, I was heartbroken and full of regret but also angry at everyone, including myself. I was angry that we'd moved up north, angry that my gran had died, and angry that I was messing up in yet another school.

In the end, I lost interest in any subjects that weren't music, drama or sports. I told myself my GCSEs in all the other subjects were going to be a washout because of the classes I was in, and I literally folded and gave up. I spent most lessons drawing pictures of horses and sticking pictures of Damon Albarn from Blur on my exercise books. The phrase rebellious teenager might be overused, but that's what I'd become, I suppose. Having moved around seven different schools, I always felt like I was starting from scratch; starting at the bottom. This was frustrating, with people always telling me how bright I was.

What's the point? I thought. Why bother to settle in and buckle down when I'll probably be uprooted soon and have to start all over again?

One lunchtime, I walked out of the school gates and went to the chippy with some mates, and it suddenly dawned on me that I just couldn't face going back inside the gates. So, instead of heading back to lessons, I walked home after lunch break was over.

Mum was there when I got home, wondering what on earth I was doing back home so early, probably imagining I was ill or something.

'What are you doing here?' she asked.

'I'm not going back, Mum,' I said. 'I'm done with it.'

Digging my heels in about not attending school caused a lot of stress within the family, especially with my dad not being around much. The school even got social services involved, but nothing seemed to work. It was even suggested that I go in once or twice a week, just to keep up my studies.

'What's the point?' I said. 'Because I started late, I couldn't take half the options I wanted to take, and I'm stuck in the lower grades.'

In the end, I did nothing at all. I was sitting around on my arse, desperate to go to performing arts college full time, which wasn't an option because I was only fifteen.

Looking back, I feel guilty for what I must have put my mum through. One minute she was dealing with a kid who was super energetic, and the next I was too tired to do anything at all. It was a real struggle for her, and what made it worse was that, with Dad away, she was doing a lot of the worrying on her own. As well as that, the marriage was strained. It must have been an incredibly difficult time, and I wasn't making things any easier.

For me, the worst part about moving from school to school so many times was how very hard it was to form friendships that lasted. I might make a friend or two at one school, but then I'd have to start all over again at the next. I think, because of that, I have always been a little socially awkward, which sometimes made being famous and in the public eye hard for me.

You might imagine that it would have made fame easier, continually meeting new people and going into new situations. However, for me, it had the opposite effect. I also feel that it affected my ability to make and keep friends. After all I've done and all the situations I've been through within Girls Aloud, I can probably count my real friends on one hand. I'm sure that's the case with many people my age, but at one time I had seemingly countless friends. Some of them just drifted away, as is the case with certain friends over the years, but there are also others who took advantage of my friendship, and who weren't real friends at all.

CHAPTER THREE

These days my concentration is all over the place; my mind feels like it's everywhere. It's almost like being back at school again; not being able to concentrate in class. In fact, even sitting down to watch a movie can take an enormous amount of concentration. I think it's all to do with the treatment and what it does to me: the chemo, the steroids, all of it. What's worse is that we're in lockdown and I have to be extra vigilant. I can hardly go out of the house or do anything. So, on top of everything else, I'm bored. At the moment, concentrating on stories from the past is something to focus on, rather than cancer, MRIs, CAT scans, radiotherapy, blood tests, not to mention all the various pills I have to take.

As well as the prescribed medical treatment, I've been keen to try out alternative therapies too; not as a replacement for traditional medicine, but as something that can go hand-in-hand with it. I've always been a big believer in the power of the mind and the power of healing, so it can't hurt, right? Things like Reiki and CBD oil, which you can get at most health store-based pharmacies, are both things I've tried during this time. My friend Duncan James from Blue was the one who suggested I try CBD oil. He'd used it after he suffered a massive back injury, while he was doing drag and wearing heels in the UK tour of *Priscilla, Queen of the Desert*. The poor guy ended up in so much pain, almost paralysed down his left side. In fact, he almost died when fluid from his brain leaked out of a surgical wound. I figured that if it was something that could help Duncan in that situation, then I should definitely give it a go. Duncan's been an absolute angel since my diagnosis went public, sending me lots of voice messages and words of support and encouragement.

Towards the end of my time at school, everyone gave up on trying to make me go. I was only interested in sports, music and drama, so perhaps that was the way forward. I'd had a spell attending Stagecoach performing arts classes when I was younger, where, among other things, I'd got to act in a production of *Bugsy Malone*, playing Tallulah. I was good at it, I enjoyed it, and I wanted to do more of it. So, instead of going back to school, I went to North Cheshire Theatre School, part-time, which scratched my wannabe performer itch, and also kept me out of trouble.

I went on Mondays, Wednesdays and Fridays, doing dance, acting and singing. The singing classes included lots of gospel singing, which I adored; the blend of different voices within the various groups and the harmonising really appealed to me. I'd never thought about singing in a group before; all I knew was that I loved singing, and the idea of becoming a professional singer.

One of the things I discovered at theatre school was that dance wasn't for me. I should have known really. When I was very young, Mum took me to ballet and tap classes, but in the end, she had to pull me out of them because I was a nightmare. I always wanted my mum to stay and watch and even join in the classes, and hated her leaving me there. Once she'd gone, more often than not, I'd end up throwing a tantrum and causing mayhem in the class. I guess not much has changed since then; I'm still a bit of a tantrum queen sometimes.

Anyway, the dance classes at North Cheshire Theatre School were equally challenging. I may not have been lying on the floor, but I just couldn't seem to get to grips with choreography. Most of the other pupils had danced all their lives, and I was so far behind them, it seemed pointless. I was certainly nothing like my future bandmates Cheryl or Kimberley in that respect: Cheryl had attended the Royal Ballet's summer school, at the age of nine, and Kimberley had also gone to theatre school, singing and dancing from a young age. Even down the line, when I was in Girls Aloud, it wasn't unusual for me to have a meltdown while we were all trying to learn the choreography, which there was plenty of.

Luckily, in Girls Aloud we had the most fantastic choreographer in Beth Honan. She worked with us from very early on in our careers. She's gone on to become the most amazing creative director. Beth always knew how to handle me. Like me, she has always been a bit of a tomboy, and she understood my struggle and often worked overtime with me. Sometimes I would go in an hour early to work with her before the other girls arrived, or we might carry on learning a routine through our lunch breaks; anything to help me catch up with the other girls, who were much faster at picking up Beth's sharp, slick choreography than I was.

I remember once when she was teaching me this *pas de bourrée*-type step, which is a 'back-side-front' step used in jazz dance. Beth had a unique way of helping me remember the steps by reciting the phrase 'kick that bitch, kick that bitch!' over and over as I did it. There were other funny little rhymes she gave me to remember various steps, and they would always come into my mind while I was performing. So while the rest of the girls were naturally giving it some on stage, I'd probably be muttering a memorable phrase under my breath between my singing lines. Amazingly, I never said any out loud over the mic in the middle of a song. Can you imagine that booming out over an arena? 'Kick that bitch, kick that bitch!' Everyone would have wondered what the hell was going on up there.

It was around this time in 1998 that my dad had an affair, and my parents' marriage came to an unhappy end. Although Mum tried to save it, they finally ended up divorcing in 2002. To be honest, I think she'd been trying to hold the family together for quite some time. With my dad in bands and on the road so much, she'd become a musician's widow, but when Dad left, she didn't cope too well. It was at this time that I moved out of home, which I've never forgiven myself for, because, in many ways, Mum needed me then more than ever.

I was devastated when Dad left. I missed him so much because we'd been mates, but at the same time, those feelings were all mixed up with the disappointment and anger I felt towards him. I'd tried to go on pretending everything was OK, but I found the fact that he was no longer in our lives heartbreaking and emotionally draining.

Sometime after he left, I arranged for him to visit me in Manchester. I found a bed and breakfast for him to stay in for the duration of the visit, and I was looking forward to it.

The night he got there, we went to a Chiquito Mexican restaurant in Salford Quays, and everything seemed to go OK – at least I thought it did. Dad went back to his B&B, and we planned to meet up the next day. That never happened. Dad left a note for me, which said: 'Sorry, I can't do this'.

He'd then driven back to where he lived without saying goodbye. I was still only about 17 at the time, so it was pretty hard to take.

It was only a couple of years ago when Dad finally came back into my life. I suppose by then I was ready to give him another chance. Time moves on, and we were all getting on in years. I wanted to know my family. By then, his second marriage had ended – a marriage which had given him two more sons and me two more half-brothers.

It's funny, I suddenly found myself building studios to make my music in, and wishing Dad was there to help me and share in the experience. That's the kind of thing we would have enjoyed when I was little; me hanging out in studios with him.

It was the late 1990s. I was living in my first studio apartment in Stockport, and my life was suddenly getting hectic. Aside from setting up my first home, I was working in a hair and beauty place on Saturdays, and a local nightclub. On top of that, I was delivering pizzas. Nobody could ever accuse me of expecting something for nothing, that's for sure.

It was my first real taste of freedom: my own apartment, my own car and my own money.

Having no GCSEs when I left school, further education was going to be difficult. I wanted to do a BTEC in Beauty Therapy, but that was impossible with no qualifications, so I ended up on a hair and beauty course. Looking back, I think I was hung up on wanting to be more ladylike. More like a 'proper girl', whatever that meant. I still thought of myself as a tomboy, and I wanted to be thought of as pretty. I wanted to learn how to maintain myself and how to look good. This would be especially important if I was eventually going to have a career in performing arts. I had to look the part.

While I enjoyed the beauty side of the course, I wasn't interested in the hairdressing side of things. I did do my mum's hair on occasion, and I got to do ring curls and purple rinses on a few of the grannies that came to the college for a free-do on OAP days, but that was as far as it went.

Me being me, I started to slack off on the hairdressing part of the course, instead finding myself propping up the student union bar with other girls at the college. That was always fun: taking on some of the lads on the PlayStation, eating hotdogs, and having half a shandy. I had a lot of fun hanging out there.

I never understood why I wasn't allowed to just study the thing I wanted to learn. It was all about qualifications and not having the right GCSEs. With that in mind, I wasn't always honest about what qualifications I did and didn't have after that. I managed to get a couple of jobs while being economical with the truth and still do the job perfectly well.

One of my early jobs was working for a debt collection agency. I'm not sure what qualifications I needed for that job, but I ended up getting it anyway.

In the offices, we all wore little headsets, telephoning people who were behind on their payments for one thing or another. You can just imagine the abuse we got.

I would have to say things like, 'I'm sorry, sir. If you can't pay us at least five pounds a week of your debt, I'll have to send an agent around to your door.'

'You send an agent round here, and I'll set the fucking dogs on him,' would often be the type of reply I'd get back.

I always tried to go for the softer approach, suggesting a manageable financial agreement before mentioning the bailiff. Still, I'd often be accused of threatening people.

'What kind of customer service do you call this?' an angry caller once said to me.

What I wanted to say was, 'This ain't bloody customer service, mate; you're in debt,' but of course I could not.

During rare quiet periods at the agency, we'd sit at our desks, flicking rubber bands at one another. There was one hilarious guy called Dave, who always tried to inject humour into his calls, slipping in witty puns depending on people's names.

'I'm sorry, Mr Brush, but you can't just sweep your problems under the carpet,' was one I remember laughing about.

God, the jobs I had. I worked for 192 Directory Enquiries, and at All Sports … I even delivered car parts in a Citroën Berlingo van. I certainly wasn't a person who expected things to fall in her lap, because that wasn't how I'd been raised. I learned, from a very young age, that I had to work hard for everything that came my way. At one point, I was working four different jobs, just so I had enough to cover the considerable costs of living in my studio apartment. That place gave me independence, and I didn't want to have to give it up. Looking back, living on my own wasn't all it was cracked up to be back then. My apartment was in the middle of Stockport, just off the A6, right at the top of the building. It was tough going. Still, I was free to come and go as I pleased, which, after being at boarding school for so much of my child-hood, was a luxury.

My girlfriends would come over of an evening, and we'd swig Lambrusco while we were getting all dolled up to go out on the town. Our nights usually started at Grand Central bar, which we called the 'Granny Bar'. That was followed by another bar called Lucky's. Finally, a club called Heaven & Hell, once famously known as Volts, which played club/dance mixes downstairs 'in hell', and fabulous cheesy pop music upstairs 'in heaven'. It was the best of both worlds. One of my extra little jobs during the week was flyering for that particular club, so I usually managed to get us all in for free, which, of course, was a bonus.

For a time, I also worked at a pub called the Legh Arms in Prestbury, which was, and still is, a charming old-fashioned village pub, serving good food. I worked behind the bar, brought food to the tables and generally got to know the locals. In fact, I had great banter with a lot of the old boys who used to come in and order their pints of bitter – they all seemed to love me.

It was here that I met two people who both became a big part of my life.

One of them was Fran, who also worked behind the bar. We worked a lot of our shifts at the Legh Arms together, getting up to all sorts of mischief and having a giggle. Fran's sister Nat worked in a place called Nice Bar, which was next door to the pub, so one of us was always sneaking across to say hello while the other covered the shift.

We both loved gossiping and having a laugh with the old boys who came drinking at the Legh. We could often be found trying to get them to sample something a tad more exotic than their customary pints of bitter, lager or Guinness.

'Why not try a B-52 shot, lads!'

As you may know, a B-52 is a triple-layered shot made of Kahlua, Baileys and Grand Marnier, and not for the faint-hearted. Apparently, it's named after the American band rather than the World War Two bomber!

Some of the guys really got the taste for it. They'd come into the bar after finishing their dinner and order a coffee, and I'd ask, 'Would you like a little short one with that?' Then I'd set about making the shots and lining them up on the bar. You put the coffee liqueur in, then pour the Baileys over a spoon to make the next layer, and finally the Grand Marnier. The shot ends up with three distinct layers, which you can then light.

From then onwards, Fran and I stayed close friends. She's one of those people who knew me before I was famous and has remained the same throughout. One of those rare people where, even if I don't see her for a while, nothing really changes. There have been times over the years when we haven't been in touch, and life has got in the way, but the minute we speak, it's as if no time has passed.

She has a baby now, Beau, who is unbelievably cute, but our friendship goes all the way back to those days at the Legh Arms, pouring B-52 shots for the old boys at the bar.

I also set up my now single mum with one of the lovely men who frequented the Legh; a man named Peter, who I got on brilliantly with. I didn't know it then, but he was also to be an important person in my life. Peter was a fair bit older than Mum, but I somehow knew that they'd hit it off. It started with Peter regularly coming into the bar, and me having his pint of bitter and his peanuts in a bowl on the bar, all ready for him. He'd been a fighter pilot in the RAF, and fought in the Malayan war, so always had plenty of life experience to share.

One evening, Peter and a few of the lads were at the bar, laughing and joking with me, as they did.

'Do you know anyone who's single, Sarah?' he asked. 'Some of us could do with meeting some single women.'

'Well, my mum's single, but that's about it,' I said, with a grin.

Later, Peter came over to talk to me across the bar.

'Hey, Sassy!' That was his nickname for me. 'I think I'd quite like to meet your mum.'

'Well, you can because she's coming in tomorrow,' I said, suddenly hatching a plan. 'I'll introduce the two of you.'

Peter booked a table for lunch in the pub, and, the next thing I knew, the meeting had turned into a lunch date between him and my mum. While it was happening, I was like some kind of Peeping Tom, sneaking glances at them through the windows of the restaurant section, just to make sure it was all going to plan.

From then on, Mum and Peter became close. I'm not sure they ever put a tag on their relationship as far as definitions go. Still, they were constant companions, going on holidays to Lanzarote and doing everything together. They shared so much of their lives, and it was wonderful to see.

Peter was my pal. Always on hand to give me advice and to talk when I needed to. 'Now, Sassy, listen to your old pal, Peter,' he used to say whenever he was about to impart words of wisdom. He became something of a cross between a grandfather, uncle and surrogate dad to me – a truly wonderful man.

He passed away four years ago, after living in a very nice care home for a short time, leaving an enormous gap in our family and in my life. While sorting through some boxes recently, I found Peter's old RAF cap. I must have had it for years, and finding it again made me feel so proud of him. He was a real character and I miss him loads, as does Mum. He and Mum were companions right up to the very end.

The best thing about moving to Manchester was the vibrant music scene. That's when I really started getting into music seriously.

I loved its escapism. I knew some friends thought I was over the top and crazy, but I didn't care. I just had this confidence when it came to music that seemed to come out of nowhere, and I didn't care what anyone thought about me.

As far as advancing my career in singing went, I wasn't really sure how to go about it. I didn't have any experience with auditions. I guess it was because Mum wasn't one of those eager show-biz types that could get me into things like that; it just wasn't her world. That said, Mum is convinced that music is in my blood and she's probably right. As I mentioned, my paternal grandmother was a classically trained pianist, and my maternal grandmother sang and played piano too. Also, two of Mum's cousins were very much in demand on the northern entertainment scene for both acting and singing.

However, not coming from any kind of formal theatrical background, apart from having my dad as a musical mentor, I was also clueless about the audition process or even what was out there. The first crack at performing in front of an audience, aside from productions at school and at performing arts, came from singing karaoke in pubs.

One of the girls on my performing arts course was in a girl band, and her older brother acted as her manager. One night, he came and watched me singing in one of my regular karaoke pubs, and made an offer to sign me up. I ended up regularly travelling to Rhyl in Wales, where I'd perform in pubs, doing two 45-minute sets. I got paid £45, which, after paying for the PA and petrol, left me with the princely sum of £15. I guess that was my apprenticeship; driving to North Wales and singing in the pubs and caravan parks. It was really my first step to becoming a performer.

Project G was the name of my friend's girl band, and I was invited to be part of it. We did some demos, but two of the girls in the band were at college and couldn't commit, so that didn't last long. Still, the management company kept me on, recording some dance tracks, which I enjoyed. DJ Dave Pearce was interested in one of the tracks I did, and it was exciting when he played it on his show on Radio One. Still, my career as a dance-diva was to be short-lived because it all happened around the time when *Popstars: The Rivals* was starting. That ended up taking over, particularly as I got further and further along in the competition. But hey, I'm jumping ahead of myself!

There were a few 'almost there' and near-miss moments in my early career. At one point, I even signed a contract to record dance tracks for an Italian record label. The trouble was, I had no idea what the music sounded like because they wouldn't play it to me before I got there. In the end, I managed to pull out of the contract with my brother's help. I also nearly ended up in the group Sweet Female Attitude, who went on to have a hit with 'Flowers'. Unfortunately, I had to have my tonsils out, so that plan was also scuppered. That's another weird thing about me – my bloody tonsils. I'd already had them out once when I was seven. By some freakish circumstance, however, they'd grown back over the years. After complaining of a sore throat for the longest time while I was at the hair and beauty college, doctors told me that I'd been in a constant state of tonsillitis for about a year; my bloody tonsils had grown back. I should have been in *X-Men*, I tell you. Tonsil woman! Or *Deadpool 2*, when Wade Wilson's lost legs grow back as baby legs, and he has to learn to walk on them all over again.

A couple of years after that I went up for a show called *Fame Academy*, which was like the BBC alternative to *Pop Idol*. The only trouble with that was it seemed to be full of people who wrote their own songs and played their own instruments, so I wasn't convinced I was the right fit.

Around the same time, there was another big TV competition about to start: *Popstars: The Rivals*. The first series in the *Popstars* franchise, the previous year, had been huge, producing Hear'Say. Also two major artists, Will Young and Gareth Gates, had broken out of the *Pop Idol* franchise. This sounded much more like the kind of thing I'd be suited to. Perhaps this would be my chance to shine.

CHAPTER FOUR

The apartment I wanted has been approved and I have a moving date. It's all going well and I can't wait. It's not going to be easy, I know that. I'm not sure that I'm going to be able to cope on my own. The idea is for Mum to come and stay with me while I settle in. It's funny, really, and quite sad. I've lived on my own since I was a teenager, and I've always known how to look after myself. Having this disease takes more away from a person than just their health. It takes away their independence and their sense of self. Things that once seemed so easy have suddenly become a mountain for me. Things I once took for granted – simple everyday things – now feel like pots of treasure that are somehow out of reach. I suppose that's why getting this place is so important to me, and why I've really pushed my lawyer Tricia to make it happen. The relative normality of being back in my own home, living with my dogs, is all I can think about because it's about moving forward. It's about the future. My future.

For now, though, let's get back to the past.

Back in the early 2000s, the men's magazine *FHM* had a feature called High Street Honeys, which came in the form of a free booklet to accompany the magazine. It was, as the name suggests, pictures of everyday women, who weren't models or even famous, in sexy, sultry poses. It was 2002, and around the time that I'd started to feel a bit more confident in myself. I'd gone from tomboy to young woman, and I guess I wanted people to see the new me.

I did a photoshoot with my boyfriend at the time. I wasn't naked, and the pictures weren't crass or tasteless, and I made it into *FHM*'s top ten High Street Honeys. However, the publication just happened to coincide with me getting the audition for *Popstars: The Rivals*, which seemed much more exciting to me than the idea of being a model. I looked pretty good, sitting in a car wearing nothing but a St George's flag under the caption: 'Doing It For England'. Still, when it came to a choice between singing and having my photo taken, singing was always going to win out.

Unsurprisingly, these photos did surface down the line, and God, did I look young and fresh-faced in them. I've still got a set of them somewhere. There was also one of me wearing hot pants in a phone box, which was very kitsch.

When it came down to it, I was quite uncertain about auditioning for *Popstars: The Rivals* – scared, I suppose, that I was going to make a fool of myself in front of millions of TV viewers. It was an ex-boyfriend who talked me into going for it in the end, literally on the night before the audition. So off I went to the Lowry Hotel in Manchester where the auditions were being held.

When I finally got through the door, it wasn't at all what I'd imagined at first. I ended up in a line of about ten people in a room, singing in front of some TV producers and someone from a record company. Once I'd managed to get through that stage, it was time to sing in front of the cameras and the judges: Pete Waterman, Geri Halliwell and Louis Walsh. For my audition, I wanted to sing a big ballad, like 'I'll Be There', which is the type of song that always went down well when I did karaoke. The show's presenter, Davina McCall, was telling everyone to make sure they had a backup song. Still, I couldn't think of anything else I wanted to sing. When the judges said they wanted me to sing something more pop, I started singing 'Last Thing On My Mind' by Steps. I knew I'd have sounded much better doing Mariah, but that it was best to give the judges what they wanted. I was so nervous, I veered off-key slightly, but I held my nerve and got through it. At the end of it, Pete Waterman said, 'You're through; you're going to London.' I blew the judges a kiss and said, 'Thank you!' And that was it: I was on my way.

Unfortunately, my nerves continued throughout the show. Even as I made it through, week after week, I still found the whole process of a TV talent show really tough. The choreography was a particular nightmare for me. Try as I might to learn all the steps, the minute I felt like there were eyes on me, I seemed to go to pieces. As each week rolled around, I just carried on regardless, muddling through and winging it as best I could. At no time did I really let myself believe that I was going to end up in the band's final line-up because I didn't want to set myself up for a fall. At the end of each week, when I got through to the next round, I'd think,

Oh, OK! Maybe I'm not as bad as I think I am. Then as the next week rolled around, the nerves would start all over again.

To say that I was surprised to get into the final ten was an understatement.

The final ten contestants all ended up living in a house together, but that wasn't easy for me. I'd never had a sister or hung around girls a lot since my boarding school days, so being suddenly thrust into a situation where I was living with nine of them was a bit of a shock. It's funny: I can be quite shy in certain situations, but the other side of me is the absolute opposite. Sometimes in the house, I was rather loud and over the top, and it soon became apparent that I wasn't everyone's favourite housemate. I ended up feeling quite disconnected from the rest of the girls, crying myself to sleep because I didn't feel like I fitted in – and I so wanted to.

The performance side of the show was no better for me. I didn't like the way I was styled half the time, and I rarely enjoyed the song choices. In the end, I spoke up and said that I wanted to choose my own song and that I wanted to do my own hair and make-up. That was the one week on the show I felt happy with myself, finally singing Mariah's version of 'I'll Be There'.

When the final line-up of the band was announced, and the other four girls had been chosen, it came down to Javine Hylton and me. The whole thing was horribly nerve-wracking and emotional. Presenter Davina McCall brought us out front and told us how surprised she was that we were the last two to be picked. On the judging panel, Geri Halliwell said that the two of us had pulled the best performances out of the bag and that either one of us could easily have a solo career. This might have been the case, but at the time all I could think about was how much I wanted this. After what felt like an agonisingly long ad break, my mum was brought down out of the audience, in readiness to console me, live on stage, if I lost the vote.

Then Davina announced the name of the last girl who was to join the band: 'Sarah'.

Of course, I burst into tears and sobbed on Javine's shoulder. I was utterly overcome at being chosen, because, in truth, the expectation was that Javine was one of the dead-certs to be picked. To be honest, some of my tears were because I wasn't sure all the rest of the girls were so happy with the choice. I know we all feel very different about it now, and that the girls are delighted the way things turned out, but at the time I felt like they would have preferred Javine to complete the line-up, simply because some of them had become good mates with her. When I sat down with the rest of the girls, Davina announced our name to the world: 'Girls Aloud'.

The truth is the name Girls Aloud had only been decided the night before the announcement of the band's final line-up. For an entire week before that, we were simply 'Aloud'. Other names on the shortlist list had been Overdose, Raw NV, X-Quizit, Raw Class, Raw Mix, Raw Deal and Raw Silk. It's hard to imagine any of these now, but they were all serious contenders at the time. The record company even tried to register Raw Silk – and everyone, including ITV, had signed off on this being our name. However, it turned out there was another band with that name, so the registration application was declined. X-Quizit, on the other hand, turned out to be the name of a porn site!

To add to my insecurity about making the final line-up, there were stories in the media the next day that really took the wind out of my sails. Some papers ran with reports that the vote was fixed, and it should have been Javine that made the line-up rather than me. There were even stories of viewers who said they'd voted for Javine and then got a text back saying they'd voted for me – that it was a fix. It wasn't great for my confidence. Journalists who write those stories, and the people who go online commenting about them, don't realise how upsetting it can be, and what it does to a person's aspirations and confidence. This was something I'd worked towards for such a long time, and now some people were saying I didn't deserve it. So, rightly or wrongly, I started off my whole Girls Aloud journey feeling slightly unwanted.

The whole idea behind 'The Rivals' idea was the race to see which band would be number one for Christmas. It was us against the chosen boy band, One True Voice. They were mentored by Pete Waterman while we were looked after by Louis Walsh and affiliated to Polydor Records. We mounted a huge campaign, almost like a political campaign, using the slogan 'BUY GIRLS, BYE BOYS!' and we tried to get it out everywhere, in every way we could. Wherever we went, up and down the country, we'd be handing out flyers. Even when our people carrier was stopped at a traffic light, we'd be chucking out flyers to anyone we could reach.

The majority of the media decided to back One True Voice. I'm not sure why; maybe it was because they felt that the female audience would be the more significant audience and naturally go for a bunch of cute guys. It felt like everyone was more interested in interviewing the boys than they were us. In fact, try as they might, Polydor couldn't get us a slot on Capital Radio, while the boys were invited with open arms. Still, we weren't going to let a little thing like that stop us, so our guy at Polydor, Peter Loraine, along with Poppy Stanton and his marketing team, came up with a fabulously wicked plan. During the radio show when One True Voice were in as guests, Polydor bought all the advertising slots around their interview, with *Popstars'* host Davina McCall voicing over our 'Buy Girls, bye boys' slogan. It was genius.

Smash Hits magazine also said they were backing the boys, and put them on the front cover. All the way along, the tide seemed to be against us. I suppose that's what made us even more determined.

Peter later told us that one of the Polydor managing directors had given carte blanche for him to pull out all the stops.

'I don't care what you do or what you spend, just make sure we win,' he said. The Bee Gees were also signed to Polydor, so Peter heard on the grapevine that the One True Voice single was to be a cover version of 'Sacred Trust' – a Bee Gees track. Peter thought it would be fun for us to record our own version of the same song, so when you bought the CD single of our record 'Sound of the Underground', you also got 'Sacred Trust' into the bargain as a bonus track. He wanted to put a sticker on the CD that said, 'also includes "Sacred Trust"'.

As much as they wanted to win, this particular plan was deemed a step too far for the bosses at Polydor, who felt like we were playing too dirty, so in the end it never happened.

At the end of the day, I think the reason we won came down to the way we were presented and the fact we had an amazing launch single. One True Voice came out with a cover version that was very typical boy band, and the production wasn't exactly edgy. In contrast, 'Sound of the Underground' was an in-your-face pop track with a great team of producers behind it – Brian Higgins, Miranda Cooper and Xenomania. It had tons of gusto and felt brand new. I loved it as soon as I heard it, particularly the drum and bass feel of the rhythm section. It was kick-ass, and like nothing you'd ever heard from a girl band. Yes, we were aiming for the Christmas number one, and this track was the least Christmassy song you could imagine; I just think we were fortunate that the team behind us had their finger on the pulse as far as what was going on in pop music. Doing it the way we did it gave us the girls vote as well as the boys; had we been dancing around in floaty dresses singing a ballad, I think it might have been a different story.

With our first single being released imminently, the video for 'Sound of the Underground' had to be shot almost immediately. I wanted to be excited, I wanted to be happy, but the whole drama around the voting made that impossible. The night before the shoot, I got hardly any sleep at all. As I sat in the Winnebago, waiting to go on to the set, I kept seeing and hearing the news stories, reporting on the so-called voting scandal. It was tough to keep my head up that day. I cried to myself until I was sick of crying.

In the end, I decided that the only way I was going to get through this was to prove to myself and everyone that I bloody well did deserve to be in Girls Aloud.

I *was* good enough.

CHAPTER FIVE

When 'Sound of the Underground' debuted at number one on 22 December 2002, it was the best Christmas present I could have dreamed of. How was this possible? I was in a band who were at the top of the charts. It just seemed insane and so hard to take in. God, we were actually going to be on *Top of the Pops*. That in itself was mind-blowing. We ended up staying at the top of the charts for four weeks, sailing into 2003. In the end, it went on to sell just short of a million copies.

Our debut album of the same name was a bit of a mish-mash of tracks written by a variety of writers, produced and recorded in a hurry. There was even a song written by Brian from Westlife called 'Girls Allowed'. This was shoe-horned on to the album, mainly because Westlife were also managed by Louis Walsh, who was our manager. Still, our second single 'No Good Advice' debuted at number two in the charts, just beaten to number one by 'Ignition' by R. Kelly, and although it didn't quite have the chart life that our first single did, it was a big hit. I loved the song because it encompassed the same attitude as 'Sound of the Underground'. We'd made our mark as a band who weren't just a bunch of pretty girls with pleasant voices; we had something to say, and we were saying it loud.

Still, it was never going to be easy to sustain that initial success. 'Sound of the Underground' was number one for a month, and we'd broken all sorts of chart records with that release; one of them was being the fastest any band had gone from formation to a number one single. That's quite some tall order to follow up.

It's no bad reflection on the other girls to say that I didn't fit in at the start of the band – and for quite some time afterwards. Sometimes, I felt like a cartoon character rather than a pop star. We were all different, but I was always the one who stuck out like a sore thumb. I was louder, brasher and said and did things in the moment. While everyone else tried their best to be professional, I was just winging it. I didn't know how to be anything other than myself, and my condition meant that I didn't always have a filter. I'm sure there were times when this was hard for the rest of the band. I know my hyperactiveness didn't always go down well. Sometimes people saw my enthusiasm as attention-seeking, but, more often than not, I was just trying to get all my thoughts out on to the table.

I'd be like, 'Ooh! Ooh! I've got an idea,' and then I'd jump on to the next thing and the next, full of beans and going nineteen to the dozen. I was like the kid in a classroom who stuck her hand up every time the teacher asked a question, shouting, 'I know the answer, I know the answer!' even though they sometimes don't!

Feeling I had to fight hard to find my place in the band, I probably pushed myself forward more than I needed to. It's something I can see looking back, but at the time, I just wanted to be accepted. From the girls' point of view, I felt I came across as loud and annoying. It didn't help that I alienated myself from the rest of them because of the way I felt. While the others were all getting along and sharing flats together, I was living on my own. We all lived in a place called Princess Park Manor; a smart, gated estate in North London. Here, Cheryl shared a place with Nicola and Nadine with Kimberley. I convinced myself I was on my own because I didn't want to be the third wheel in either one of those situations. Because I'd already lived in my own place before being in the band, I was accustomed to being by myself. In some ways, it suited me. Instead of a flatmate, I got two cats – Marley and Phoenix. They were great to cuddle up to, brilliant company, and best of all, they didn't answer back.

Princess Park Manor was known as 'Pop Star Heights' because so many pop bands and people in the industry lived there. Busted and McFly were there at the same time as us, as well as a few footballers, including the man that ended up being Cheryl's husband, Ashley Cole. The place was full of faces you recognised.

I moved around a couple of times in the complex, but my first flat was right above the gym. Once, while I was back at my mum's, somebody who supposedly worked for the complex called to tell me that there had been a fire in the gym. Apparently, it was so bad that there had been significant smoke damage in my apartment. Lying on my mum's sofa, I burst into tears, only to hear giggling in the background. The next thing I knew, Cheryl and Nicola were on the end of the line, telling me that it was their idea of an April Fool.

While I was crying, they were pissing themselves laughing. They were always a nightmare when it came to practical jokes, those two.

In those early days, we all used to travel back home a lot. Cheryl and I had the same car – a Toyota RAV4. Cheryl's was black and mine silver. We'd always head back to London on a Sunday night, ready for whatever Girls Aloud work we had on Monday morning. Sometimes, we would catch one another en route back, waving at each other as we passed. Once one of us had spotted the other, it would be a competition to see who could get back to Princess Park Manor first.

During that whole period, I was seeing Mikey Green, who'd been one of the contestants on *Popstars: The Rivals* in the boys' camp. He'd got into the last ten for One True Voice but never made it into the final line-up. The five boys who never made it actually went on to form the band Phixx. They also got a record deal and ended up lasting longer than One True Voice, having several Top 20 hits. Mikey and I were happy for the most part, like two peas in a pod. Still, before Phixx took off, which was quite a few months after the TV show ended, there were aspects of our relationship that were hard.

I was finding it tough being in the band and would often return from work feeling low. Mikey found that hard to deal with. As far as he was concerned, I'd won my place in the band who'd ultimately triumphed on the TV show, and was now a bona fide pop star, which is what he'd always dreamed of being. Mikey couldn't understand why I was so unhappy, and it was hard for me to make him understand. Being in Girls Aloud back then was a double-edged sword for me; it was the best of things and the worst.

After about a year, I really hit rock bottom. I was dreading going into work, feeling isolated and insecure, and on top of that, my relationship with Mikey suddenly hit a bit of a rough patch. Instead of enjoying everything that was there for the taking, I just wanted to stay in bed with the cats. I needed time away from everything to re-set and look after my mental health. Mikey kept reminding me how grateful I should be for all I had. However, when you're dealing with anxiety or depression, someone else telling you how wonderful your life is doesn't make the slightest bit of difference. In the end, I asked our tour manager to drive me home for a few days, back to Manchester. After a few days away, I came back with a new sense of purpose. Yes, I was still a little on edge and fragile, but I decided to throw myself into work and get on with the job of building a career. The only way I was going to survive was to do what I was good at – singing and performing.

As time went on, of course, the girls began to accept the way I was. I suppose they got used to me and saw the good parts of Sarah as well as the 'difficult' Sarah. Once they understood me and how I was, things started to operate better, but that took a while. We were several years into the band by the time I began to feel a bit more at ease with it all.

One of the things I struggled with was the idea of 'fame'. I know it's many people's dream to achieve fame, but once I'd achieved it, I realised it wasn't really mine. Don't get me wrong, I wanted success, but that was more about being recognised for doing something I was good at, rather than the celebrity of it. In fact, I didn't enjoy the attention at all, particularly given all the crap that popped up in the press about me every now and again. A particularly low moment was when one of my exes – the boy who'd persuaded me to go for the *Popstars* audition – sold topless pictures of me to the press. They were just pictures of me on the beach on holiday, but I couldn't believe he'd done it. I could laugh off most of the ridiculous stories about me that I'd seen, but that one hurt; I felt utterly betrayed.

With the release of our third single, something shifted. 'Life Got Cold' was much slower and moodier than the first two singles had been. I suppose it was a bit of a risky release, and although we all liked it, there didn't seem to be the same amount of excitement or buzz around it.

The song went into the charts at number three and ended up staying in the Top 75 for nine weeks. It was a hit, for sure, but a far cry from the success of our first two singles, especially when you consider that our first record spent 21 weeks in the chart – almost half a year! The album also hadn't shifted as many copies as everyone had imagined it might, so, after just a few months, things started to look a bit dodgy for the band. In fact, at one point Polydor wasn't even sure if there was going to be a second album at all. For the first time in a long while, the future wasn't looking quite so bright.

After 'Life Got Cold', the song 'Some Kind of Miracle' was tipped to be a single. It was another Xenomania song – co-written by Edele from the band B*Witched. None of us was all that keen on this as a single. Just in time, an opportunity to record 'Jump' – a cover of The Pointer Sisters' big hit – for the *Love Actually* soundtrack came about. Had this not happened and we'd proceeded with 'Some Kind of Miracle', our career might have been a lot shorter than it ultimately was.

The video for 'Jump' was changed at the last minute when the film people asked us to link it to the movie. Initially, it was going to be us girls, in a car, just driving in front of a screen with lots of footage behind us. Thank goodness it changed. Mind you, Hugh Grant was very choosy over which bits of the film featuring him were allowed in the video.

The up-tempo energy of 'Jump' seemed to put us back where we needed to be, and the fact that it was on the soundtrack to one of the year's biggest films was even better. The movie premiere was a real highlight for us. I'd walked that red carpet many times in my imagination, and the real thing was no disappointment. There were flashing cameras and fans screaming our names. It felt surreal and fantastic – like we'd really arrived.

For our second album, *What Will the Neighbours Say?*, it was decided that Brian Higgins and Miranda Cooper of Xenomania should write and produce the whole album. After all, they'd come up with all the best songs on the first album. The relationship with Brian wasn't the easiest at the start, because we didn't always have the same vision for us as he did. Brian was like a quirky musical genius, and quite forthright in his opinions. In fact, at times, he could be quite blunt. I liked to get my ideas across, and I was never backward in coming forward either. That didn't always make for a smooth working environment. As time went on, however, I think mutual respect developed between Brian and the band. He began to recognise our talent and our input, and we started to accept and appreciate his honesty.

Along with Miranda, he developed this smart, original sound with quirky lyrics and often unconventional song structures. I think that's what set us apart from other pop bands who stuck to a more formulaic route. With a Girls Aloud record, you never quite knew what you were going to get or where it was going to next. The only thing you could be sure of was that it was going to be bloody catchy, and never dull.

The first set of recording sessions produced the songs 'The Show', 'Androgynous Girls', 'Wake Me Up' and 'Deadlines and Diets'. Immediately the record company knew that 'The Show' was to be the lead single. They wanted to keep the mood up like we'd done with 'Jump', rather than going back to the moodier 'Life Got Cold' vibe.

The album came out in November 2004, and not long afterwards we performed 'The Show' on *The Royal Variety Performance*. The album also included 'Jump' and 'Love Machine', and was a massive Christmas seller, going double platinum. Also included on the album was the song 'I'll Stand By You', a cover version of The Pretenders original, which we recorded as the official Children In Need single. The song from the album I most loved was 'Wake Me Up'. That song, I felt, was more 'me' than some of the others. It had a rocky feel, and I guess it appealed to my inner 'rock chick'. I remember that, throughout the album campaign, I kept asking, 'Will "Wake Me Up" ever be a single?' It ended up being the fifth single from the album, reaching number four in the charts. For the video, we were on motorbikes hurtling along a highway against a desert night sky, with me wearing these fantastic studded black jeans. I have no idea where many of my Girls Aloud costumes are, but I've definitely still got those trousers somewhere! It was back in the days when we were still a little bit edgy and alternative, before all the stylists came in and it was glamour all the way. The other great thing was that there wasn't so much choreography in the video, which was always a bonus for me, as I had the most trouble with it. The rocky strains of 'Wake Me Up' suited my voice, and consequently, I got my fair share of solo lines on the track as well.

We also recorded a cover of Chris Isaak's 'Wicked Games' around that time. It was going to be a single, but for some reason it was pulled at the last minute. It's never been heard anywhere and none of us even have a copy of the recording. The video was even planned and signed off; it was meant to be a Bruce Weber-style black and white affair. Of course, that never happened either.

One of the biggest singles, of course, was 'Love Machine' – it's as catchy as hell and has become a party favourite. The funny thing is, we all hated it when we first heard it, and we certainly didn't want it to be released as a bloody single. I remember us all march-ing into Polydor to see Colin Barlow, who was one of the MDs, and telling him that 'Love Machine' was definitely not the right single. Why couldn't we release 'Deadlines and Diets', which was more of a slow jam, but quite funky? The record company pushed back and told us to trust them, and thank God we did. The tables would reverse many years later, when we insisted 'The Promise' was a single, when the label wanted to lead with 'The Loving Kind'.

The one thing that didn't seem to be working out with the band was our management. Louis Walsh had managed us since our conception, but he didn't seem to have the knack with a girl band that he did with the boy bands he'd managed: Westlife and Boyzone. Looking back, I suppose he just wasn't hands-on enough to steer us in the right direction. Despite our early success, there was a lot more we could have been doing. Opportunities were being missed in the way of product endorsements and advertising. Having hit records makes you a certain amount, but when you're not writing and producing your own music, a lot of the revenue goes to the people who are.

Our team at Polydor agreed that we needed new management, and that was where Hillary Shaw came in. She had much more of a grasp on managing female artists. She'd managed Bananarama in their heyday and had recently steered Dannii Minogue through her most successful period. Peter knew Hillary well and thought she was the right person for us to work with.

Taking Hillary on meant a real shift for us. It was a whole new way of working. While everything had been a bit haphazard up until then, Hillary's team at Shaw Thing Management made sure we all had proper, printed-out schedules that we had to stick to. I have to say, it took a while to get used to that way of working, but it was a hell of a lot easier! The other thing that was great about Shaw Thing was the team of young women Hillary had on board. Her second-in-command, Angela O'Connor, was great and would often accompany us to TV performances and photoshoots. Down the line, there were others, like Jodie, Nikki and Lily (who still works for Cheryl now) who were part of the team. Hillary also brought in a vocal producer she managed called Terry Ronald. He oversaw and mixed most of our live TV performances, always making us do warm-ups before we went on. All in all, it was a lot more organised, and suddenly there were all sorts of new opportunities coming our way. Best of all was that when Hills came on board, she helped us plan and put together our first-ever live tour, What Will the Neighbours Say?

Touring and playing live was where I came alive. It wasn't just the concerts, but the whole experience of it. Being on the bus with the other girls and our team, the buzz of backstage, the dressing up and costumes – it was all kind of magical. I always immersed myself in it completely. It was a whirlwind few months on the road with a crazy, creative family – a circus troupe.

Of course, the shows themselves were the real cherry on the cake, and that's where I really came into my own. Actually, I think sometimes the other girls thought I came into my own a bit too much, too often. Something would take over me when I was out there on stage. It was like I couldn't stop myself from being the wild, lairy Sarah everyone expected me to be. During rehearsals, we'd decided between us and our director, Beth, who was going to say what and when. However, once the show was off and running, all that planning just seemed to go out of my head. I'd end up talking over the top of one of the other girls, or saying the wrong thing – it's just the way I am.

On top of that, I had to focus really hard on remembering all the routines. As I've already said, I was a singer rather than a dancer, so the choreography sometimes put me on the back foot. With all that nervous energy bubbling away, I'd get all flustered and out of breath – especially for the first couple of shows of a tour.

By the time we were a few shows in, I'd usually settled down a bit, and that was when I really started to enjoy myself. I felt strong when I was out on stage.

I became a whole new character, and I was entirely at one with her.

CHAPTER SIX

've finally moved into my new apartment, and although it's been a bit of an uphill struggle to get here, I'm pleased to be in. Right now, I'm surrounded by boxes. In fact, you've never seen so many boxes. I wish I could even begin to tell you what's in them all, but the truth is that I don't have a Scooby because they've come from a combination of different storage units that I'm finally emptying out. Of course, there are clothes, photographs, music equipment and kitchen stuff, but it's quite a shock looking around at your whole life packed in cardboard, as I am now. There's just so much of it.

In the living room, I have what might be the longest sofa in the world. The room is a decent size, so it can take it, but the fact is, it's gorgeous and was a bit of a bargain, so I had to have it.

The apartment is within a gated, private estate and has some very nice private outdoor space too. It also has a lift that goes to the upper floor. I know, an actual lift inside the apartment. It's not something that would have been on my usual list of things to have in my living space. Still, given how bad my joints have been with the chemotherapy, particularly my knees, it's a bit of a godsend. One of the most important things for me is that the place feels very zen, with beautifully designed lighting and decor. I need that right now. Best of all, though, is the fact that I feel like I'm moving forward. It's essential, given what's happening to me, that I'm pushing forward and having goals. I can't really do much in the way of work right now, so making a new home for myself, something that's mine, is my way of saying, 'I'm still here. I'm still fighting.'

For a while, Mum will be staying here with me, so there is bedding and a mattress to get sorted for her room, as well as all my things. Moving and all the things that go with it can be stressful at the best of times. When you're trying to do it with the backdrop of feeling ill and having cancer treatment, it feels like an even more mountainous task. Luckily, I have some friends who are going to help me out over the coming weekend. Guess what? There are even more boxes to bring from storage. I'm not sure how long it's all going to take to unpack, but all I can do is go at my own pace while keeping going with my treatment.

Walking around my apartment, I feel like I'm a hundred years old. Everything hurts so much. It's as if every bit of energy has been sucked out of me. On bad days, I feel like I'm struggling from room to room, trying to work out how to move with the least amount of discomfort. The other thing that's really hard to deal with is the way I look right now. The steroids I'm taking have made me bloated to the point that I hardly recognise myself. It's as if my body is not my own any more. It doesn't work in the way it should or even look how it should.

As I mentioned earlier, I was often attracted to rogues and rebels back in the day, and yes, they seemed to like me too. So you won't be surprised to hear that I dated one or two during my time in the band, or, in some cases, almost dated!

After our very first trip to the BRIT Awards, in 2003, we were invited to the Universal Music after-party. It was there I got chatting to Robbie Williams, who'd just won the Best British Male Solo Artist award. We got on really well; in fact, I felt a real connection between us. During our chat, I asked him how he dealt with the pressure of fame and celebrity, explaining how I was struggling a bit. He admitted to me that he also found it challenging and overwhelming sometimes. We spent a lovely time together, and I liked him, but I didn't think anything else of it.

A week or so later, I got a call from one of our TV team at Polydor.

'My friend Robbie wants your number,' he said.

'Who's your friend Robbie?' I answered.

'You know, Robbie.'

'Robbie who?'

'Who do you think?' he said. 'You were talking to him for ages at the Universal do.'

'Fuck off,' I said. 'Robbie Williams?'

Wow! I mean, I hadn't even been in the band that long – only a few months, in fact – and here was one of the world's biggest music stars asking for my number. This, however, was at a time when I was on/off/on/off with Mikey; at that point, we were in an 'on' period. As tempted as I might have been, I knew I couldn't respond to Robbie; it just wouldn't have been fair. So I just let it go, flattered that Robbie had at least been interested enough to ask his mate for my number.

Not long after that, we were performing on *Ant & Dec's Saturday Night Takeaway*. Robbie turned up at the ITV studios, even though he wasn't a guest on the show that week. I was surprised, to say the least, especially when he came upstairs to the dressing rooms to say hello. I even remember him trying to wangle a few minutes alone to talk to me. The rest of the girls were so excited that he'd come for a visit so it was hard to even get a look in. It's funny, when I'd been on my own with him at the Universal party, I'd felt utterly relaxed, but with the other girls in the mix, I'd reverted to feeling like an ugly duckling. So unconfident. After the show, Robbie went out to a nightclub with Kimberley and some of our dancers, but for some reason I didn't get wind of it and missed out. When I'd asked our TV promoter, Robbie's pal, what Robbie had been doing at the studios that night when he wasn't part of the show, he'd replied, 'Sarah! What do you think he was doing there?'

I regret missing out that night. I liked Robbie very much, and I'd have liked to have got to know him better then, even just as a friend. The worst part about it was hearing Kimberley telling us all what a fantastic night they'd all had. I did feel a bit gutted. I never told her or the rest of the girls that Robbie had come down to the ITV studios to see me that night. In fact, this will probably be the first they've heard about it.

Mind you, can you imagine what might have happened if I had got together with him, given both of our histories? What a couple we'd have been, tearing around town! Perhaps it was for the best, after all. Although I sometimes think I'd like to rewind, just to see what might have been.

Mikey and I stayed solid for a year or so, and then we were on/off for a while. As time went on, the bad patches started to outweigh the good, and that's when I began to feel restless. Enter Calum Best!

I always refer to Calum as my 'beautiful disaster', after the 2003 Kelly Clarkson song. We dated on and off for about two years from 2005. Calum wasn't the most straightforward guy to be in a relationship with, but when I first met him, he was a world away from the public perception of him, which was a bit of a ladies man and a rogue. Actually, I think he got a little kick out of having that reputation for a while.

Back then, I had the patience to be with a man who was always late and not always the most reliable of dates. I barely drank and drove everywhere, so did most of the legwork when it came to meeting up. At the time, Calum was living on the penthouse level of the house of Manchester City and England goalkeeper David James and his wife Tanya. They were going through a divorce at the time, so David wasn't living there; it was just Tanya and their children. Calum didn't have an entire flat, but a huge room with an en suite bathroom, which was very comfortable. At the time, Tanya had three gorgeous little Yorkshire Terriers, and, whenever I was there, Calum and I would bring them up on the bed with us and play with them.

The story of how we met and got together is a bit of a sticky one, really. At the time I was still in a relationship with Mikey, but by then the relationship was really on its last legs. If I'm honest, we were both just letting things carry on out of habit.

The night Calum and I first met, I was with the rest of the girls from the band at our very first Glamour Awards. I remember getting a glimpse of this handsome guy on another table who I thought was someone else.

'God, is that Jude Law over there?' I said to someone at our table.

I was a big fan, and if it was Jude sitting there a few tables away, I was going to have to meet him.

'That's not Jude Law,' somebody told me. 'That's Calum Best.'

Later in the evening, I was in the bathroom area, faffing about with the knee-length, diamanté-encrusted gladiator sandals I was wearing, when Calum breezed past. I said hello, and then he made some flirty comment, along the lines of, 'Oh, I'd definitely leave those on.'

I ran into him several times throughout the evening, and he made it clear he was interested. I was attracted to him right off, but I was still with Mikey. Later that night, I was in a private area of the nightclub Funky Buddha with the girls, when Alesha Dixon came to join us. She knew Calum, so I asked her what she thought.

'He's been hitting on me all night,' I said, 'and I'm not really sure what to do. I like him, but it's not as simple as that.'

I knew things weren't right between Mikey and me, and I didn't see them getting any better, but at the time we hadn't broken up. There was no getting away from the fact that flirting with Calum put me on seriously dodgy ground.

'Calum's a lovely guy,' Alesha said, 'but if you're looking for a long-term thing, I wouldn't get involved.'

As the night went on, my resolve weakened. The more I thought about my current relationship, the unhappier I felt. After a couple more drinks I thought, screw it! By then, Calum was piling on the attention, so I went and sat down with him. Engrossed in conversation, we got closer and closer until I found myself kissing him. Unbeknown to me, there was a well-known tabloid journalist nearby, and various members of the press too.

Realising we were being watched, I headed for the dance floor, and Calum followed.

Needless to say, the story of our intimate clinch was all over the press, causing a massive fight between Mikey and me. I knew what I'd done was wrong, but at the same time, neither of us were happy. I know that if I had been happy, the thought of snogging another guy in public, however handsome, wouldn't have entered my mind. After that, Calum continued to text me, daring me to go on a date with him. I kept reminding him that I had a boyfriend, but deep down, I knew I wanted to see him again.

This feeling was the wake-up call I needed, screaming at me that I wasn't in the right relationship. It wasn't all Mikey's fault either. Looking back, I should have ended my relationship with him long before, but I was scared to move on. For a long time, my relationship with him had been the one thing I was secure in. I guess I was afraid to step away and let it go, even though I knew it wasn't working any more.

When I started dating Calum, I began to feel a bit more independent; more confident in myself. It was hard for Mikey, though. Once we'd broken up, he'd packed up and left the flat, and suddenly I was officially seeing Calum. Under normal circumstances Mikey wouldn't have necessarily known. Still, Calum and I being the people we were meant that the press were all over us. Mikey couldn't have avoided seeing the two of us together, even if he wanted to. I felt terrible about that.

Calum introduced me to a whole new world, leading me to try things I'd never tried before – some good, some not so good. I do remember trying sushi for the first time with him. The only experience I'd had with it until then was when the girls had ordered some during a recording session back in the early days. At the time, no one was wildly impressed.

'Errr … it's disgusting,' someone said. 'How are you supposed to pop these bean things?'

Of course, we all grew to love it eventually.

Calum took me to Nobu on our first date, introducing me to the delights of the deluxe Bento Box. He was very much the gentleman that night; not really what I had been expecting. Afterwards, we went down to Funky Buddha in Mayfair and had a lovely time together.

As I said, I tended to take my car everywhere back then, which meant I drank little or not at all. I'd drive to meet him after Girls Aloud appeared on *Top of the Pops* or after a day's work. As time went on, that started to get tricky. The more we were seen out together, the more the press wanted shots of us together. At times, I literally had photographers climbing over the bonnet of my car as we tried to get in or out of somewhere. On those occasions, I'd be yelling through the windscreen at them, mad as hell.

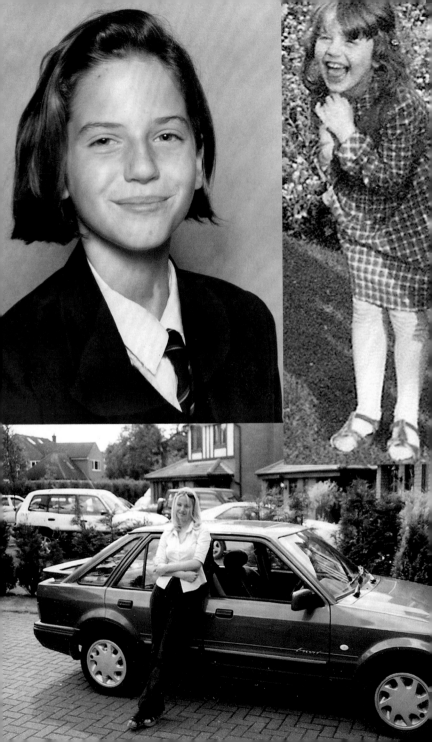

Family: My mum is still my biggest supporter!

My brother and me!

Dad and me when I was younger.

Peter, mine and my mum's good friend, always on hand to give me advice when I needed it.

My love of music is the thing that has always kept me going.

I was the last person to be announced by Davina, and I was utterly overcome at being chosen to be part of Girls Aloud. It's been a wild ride since.

I am so proud of everything
we went on to achieve.

Friends.
The ones
I'll forever
love.

'Will you lot move, please?! I can't see where I'm going! I'm trying to drive – fuck off!'

I'd been a big fan of Liam Gallagher when I was a teenager, and here I was emulating my hero, swearing at paparazzi and giving them the finger.

Calum was such a thoughtful guy at that time. Whenever I was ill, he sent flowers, and not just one bunch. Sometimes I could fill my whole kitchen with the flowers he sent. When I was very sick after catching a meningococcal infection, he even sent an enormous bunch to my mum's, where I was staying. He was the perfect gentleman, apart from the fact that he was always bloody late!

In return, I tried to be a comfort to him while his father George was dying. Calum didn't know what to do, and after his father died, I did all I could to get him out of the house because no one else could. I knew then that Calum had problems with addiction, but at the time I'd never touched drugs, so I couldn't grasp what he was going through; I just wanted him to get better.

Looking back, I think our relationship came at the perfect time for both of us. I guess Calum needed grounding and I needed to find myself and discover who I was outside of Girls Aloud. One of the things I learned from Calum was how to persevere and to be patient, which was never easy for me.

I guess meeting Calum was my gateway to the West End party scene, having fun and feeling a bit more sure of myself. It took me some time to realise that scene wasn't all it was cracked up to be, or what I'd naively imagined it would be at the start. Still, whatever happened, my time with Calum is something I look back on fondly.

CHAPTER SEVEN

bought my first flat in 2004, in Camden. It was in an old stone school building; beautiful, with vaulted ceilings, a mezzanine level and fabulously big windows. The only problem was, it all looked a bit dated, with tired-looking carpets and decor that just wasn't me. It needed a complete revamp, but having the builders there all the time got so noisy. On several occasions, I grabbed my duvet and went downstairs to sleep in my car, just so I could have a lie-in.

Still, I was never the sort of person to sit in and watch TV or knit anyway. OK, when I was in a relationship it was always nice to snuggle up to watch movies with a boyfriend. Whenever I've been single, though, I just wanted to get out there – no Bridget Jones for this girl. I just don't suit those big pants. I needed to get out there, to do stuff and to keep busy. My mind would never let me do anything other than that. It's never really been any different, whether it was ice skating, horse riding or even the few skiing lessons I had.

I'm a person who can't seem to sit still for five minutes; always on the go. I guess, because of my condition, I've always been quite a scatty person. One thought doesn't get time to finish before another one starts. I was already quite hyper as a kid, but the skittishness that developed over time came from being here, there and everywhere, and the fast pace of my life within the band. The problem I have is that people sometimes take it the wrong way. They see someone who's animated and enthusiastic and immediately assume the worst.

'She's drunk' or 'she's on drugs'.

There have been times when that kind of thing has been levelled at me when it's just not been the case. I'm not saying I wasn't a party girl and a rock 'n' roller as time went on; that's well documented. My social anxiety and eagerness to fit in led me down a few paths that maybe I shouldn't have gone down, but I've never been so out of control that I couldn't stop and pull myself back.

I'd been in circles where there'd been lots of alcohol and drugs around, long before I ever went down that road myself. In fact, I was quite naive when it came to knowing what a lot of my friends were doing when they popped off to a spare bedroom or a bathroom in pairs.

The first time I tried cocaine was at a party in Knightsbridge, in a ridiculously plush townhouse, owned by a rich Saudi playboy. The girls and I had done *Top of the Pops* that day, and later my driver had dropped me at a club to meet Calum before we headed to the house in Knightsbridge. Once we were there, Calum disappeared off with his friends. I remember sitting on a couch, on my own, feeling like a bit of a gooseberry because everyone around me was 'indulging' and I wasn't.

I knew what was going on by then, but I'd lost my cousin to drugs, and his wife too. If anything I was very anti. Calum has since talked openly about his destructive period with drugs and alcohol. Still, I suppose this was when I first started to become aware that it was happening around me.

'I know what you're up to, I'm not silly,' I told Calum when he appeared back at the party, but at the time I guess he still wasn't ready to talk to me about stuff like that.

At one point in the evening, a female friend of his warned me off.

'Listen, I know Calum better than you do. It's his way or the highway, so don't go bugging him about stuff like that.'

We ended up at the female friend's house, and, by that time, Calum was pretty messed up. Again, he was gone for ages while I just sat in the living room without a drink. I remember worrying that something was happening between Calum and his friend, as, once again, he was nowhere to be found.

In the end, I got talking to some of his friends upstairs in the living room, some of whom were indulging. I told them that Calum was off somewhere, and one of them said, 'You know what's going on; there's some over there.'

I could see the powder on the table, so I walked over and looked down at it. Fuck it, I thought, what's good for the goose and all that. One of Calum's friends was trying to persuade me not to do it, but it was like some kind of mist had descended over me.

I tried to roll up a banknote like I'd seen people do on TV and movies, but before I could finish, Calum and the female friend were behind me in the room.

'Babes, just use the straw,' she said, and she handed me one.

Calum wasn't at all happy. 'Babe, don't do it, please,' he said. 'You don't have to.'

I guess it was more bravado than anything else, but I went ahead and did it anyway. Once the deed was done, Calum got really angry.

'Thanks a lot,' he shouted at his friend. 'She was the one unspoilt, innocent thing in my life.'

'No, it's not her fault,' I chimed in. 'You lot have all been doing it every time we're out, so why shouldn't I?'

That was my first taste, and it had taken quite a while. I knew some friends who'd been doing it for years but who'd always kept it away from me because they thought I was disapproving. I suppose they were right, yet here I was at a house in Knightsbridge finally partaking. The funny thing was, there had been speculation about me doing coke even before the Girls Aloud tours. At the time, that couldn't have been further from the truth, but things change. Temptation can be hard to avoid in the entertainment industry, particularly in some of the circles I was hanging out in. There's a lot of hypocrisy involved when stories about celebrities and their drug-taking are reported in the press too. I remember hearing one male pop star say that during his drug-taking days, he'd partied with plenty of reporters and people from the media. These were probably the same reporters who wrote exposés and sensational stories about celebrities using drugs.

From there on in, I went to lots of parties like that. Luckily, I was still a bit scared of the whole drugs thing, so I never went over the top or did much of it. It was always there, though.

The problem with cocaine is that people are always chasing that first high – the one where they feel really good – or at least they think they do. It's never as powerful the second or the third time, but they keep going until they just feel nothing at all. Then it's the comedown, where they're lying in the foetal position, groaning and feeling like absolute shit.

I didn't know it that first time, but in the following years I would have some bumpy patches with both drugs and alcohol, and plenty of other times when I was strong enough to say no. The bad patches mostly came when I was using something to numb the pain of a situation – self-medicating, I guess you'd call it. These are things I'll talk about down the line, but suffice to say, after that first time something in me had changed. I'd crossed a line and, as time went on, the more I did it, the more immune to the fear I became. In the end, it felt like a natural thing to do when I went out. It was what you did when you were out partying; it was what everyone did, wasn't it?

I suppose the best thing about those days was how many fun and fabulous people I met along the way, several of whom have remained true friends. Going out opened up a whole new world for me, and I was forever meeting new people. That gave me confidence. Even some of the journalists became my mates, although I had a love-hate relationship with some of them. Often it was like a game of chess between us; a game of who could outsmart the other. Sometimes they were kind, and sometimes, if I made a wrong move, they screwed me over.

Of course, there were the inevitable times when my partying meant that I sometimes had to go to work not feeling my best. In fact, there were occasions when I went to work not having been to bed at all. Those were the days when I was 'hanging out of my arse', as the northern saying goes.

I recall one occasion when we were doing an early-ish morning interview, and I really wasn't feeling it. The woman who was conducting the interview came over a little bit snooty, which was not what I needed in my delicate state, let's put it that way. She seemed to have a problem with the fact that I wouldn't take off my Ray-Bans, but, given my condition, that simply wasn't an option. I mean, how was I supposed to keep my eyes closed without dark glasses on? Good Lord! At one point during the interview, while the girls were chattering on, I actually fell right to sleep sitting there. I'm not sure if anyone noticed, but given how chatty I usually am, I'm sure the girls must have known. God, I was tired.

Then, when I did speak, it was, 'Yeah. No. I s'pose.' Not what the journalist was hoping for from a supposedly lively, bubbly pop star, I'm sure. Still, the other girls covered for me – and not for the first time. Not surprisingly, the journalist's comments about me in the subsequent article weren't all that complimentary.

Thinking back, all of us have had our moments. There isn't a single one of Girls Aloud who hasn't had a diva strop or drama at one time or another. Usually, when it happens, one or more of the others will pull them up on it. That's the way it works in a band. We all have our bad days, and sometimes we need to be reminded what's acceptable. I've certainly had my fair share of those. Mostly, we were able to laugh about those mad moments – eventually!

We also all enjoyed a drink and a party, it wasn't just me. I guess Nadine and I were probably the girls in the band who liked a tipple most, although I probably left her in the dust most of the time. Once lockdown was over, she came up to Manchester to visit me, and we shared a glass or three of wine. Fran was here too, and later on Fran's sister and her husband came over. It was just the right amount of people for me to be able to handle. I must admit, I find being with only one person difficult right now because I'm scared of the quiet moments. Those gaps where neither of you knows what to say. I've always hated those silent moments. I guess they're less likely to happen with a small crowd all bubbling away around you. Just not too big a crowd, that's all. Not now.

The occasion that night was an early Christmas do, and not only did Nadine cook but she also cleaned up everything afterwards. She whipped up the most fabulous dinner: langoustines and scallops followed by seafood linguini. We went all out, buying a mini Christmas tree, which we decorated together, swapping presents.

Throughout the evening, we all had our moments of hysterical laugher followed by tears. At one point, Nadine told me in no uncertain terms how much she cared about me.

'You don't understand, Sarah. I love you!'

It was partially fuelled by the wine, but I also knew in my heart that she meant every word she said. I could see it in her eyes. Then Fran came into the room, and we had a group hug and all started crying together. Then we'd laugh at the fact that we were all crying. It was quite an emotional night, and the drinks made it even more so.

After everyone had gone, I sat up late into the night talking to Nadine while we ate cheese and biscuits. OK, so it wasn't like the nights of wild partying I did back in the day, but it was still very special.

CHAPTER EIGHT

NADINE
ON SARAH

vividly remember spotting Sarah for the first time, out of all the hundreds of people who were at the very first auditions for *Popstars: The Rivals*. It was the bright blonde hair; the seemingly confident air she had. She was so bubbly and loud – you couldn't have missed her if you'd tried. Growing up in a small town as I had, I'd never met anyone like Sarah before. There might just as well have been a great big sign above her head, declaring, 'This is me! I'm here!' Naturally, I just rolled my eyes and thought, oh my God; she's going to be one of those attention-seeking stage-school nightmares.

When we both got to the final ten, and all ended up living in a house together, Sarah and I ended up sharing a room. This was where I very quickly saw a different side to her – perhaps the real side.

Surprisingly reserved, Sarah is a deep thinker. In fact, she spent much of her time with her nose in a book. I noticed her language and vocabulary as well. When you were having a conversation with Sarah, she'd use all these long words and cleverly articulated sentences, unlike the rest of the girls in the house. Given what my first impression had been, I was quite struck by what I saw. Who is this girl? I thought. What's she about? It was such a surprise that this personality was hidden underneath all the overblown bravado.

The situation we were thrown into – ten young women all vying for a place in a band in which there were five spots – meant that emotions ran high much of the time. Consequently, stresses and anxieties spilt over between us in the house. Sarah had a much older brother, so she'd been raised as if she were an only child, but now here she was in a house full of showbiz siblings. A bunch of new sisters, fighting and squabbling, like sisters often do. She seemed to find it overwhelming and eventually moved to another room. I don't think it was necessarily a problem between us that made her move; it was just the whole atmosphere of our living situation. Sarah found it hard to acclimatise.

Sarah began her life in Girls Aloud with a cloud hanging over her head. She was the last to be chosen, and there was all the negative press about the choice of her over Javine. Sarah either felt like she wasn't good enough, or that other people didn't think she was good enough.

I suppose I was sort of aware of what she was going through at the time, but I was 17, four years younger than Sarah, so I wasn't really equipped to presume what she might be thinking. The enormity of what was happening to us was such that I had just about had enough brain-space to think about what I was going through. I knew Sarah didn't feel comfortable, but I didn't know what to do to make it better. To be honest, I had my own issues. I felt overworked and stressed out, as we all did. For those first few months after winning the show, all five of us were fighting to keep up with the pace, fighting to stay above water almost. I could hardly help myself, let alone somebody else.

That all changed when I went back to Ireland to visit my parents a few months after the band was formed. My mum and dad showed me a video of the moment when it was announced that I'd got into the band. When Davina announced my name, I stood up, in complete shock. At the same time, Sarah jumped up to give me a hug, but I completely ignored her and kept on walking. My mum and dad both said to me, 'Nadine, that's not right. You completely ignored that girl.'

I felt so guilty. The video showed Sarah clearly reaching out to hug me, and me ignoring her. Of course, I was in a daze at the time, having just found out my entire life was about to change, but it was still tough to watch that moment. I felt dreadful.

I realised that I hadn't even tried to make an effort with Sarah in the first couple of months of the band. I already knew that deep down she wasn't just this crazy blonde dynamo that she outwardly portrayed; that there was much more to her than that. I told myself I needed to spend some time getting to know who she really was, and from then on I made an effort to do just that.

I remember being in a car with all the girls, travelling to one of the many roadshows we did up and down the country. I sent a secretive text to Sarah, apologising for ignoring her on the night we got into the band. I knew it had to be said, but I didn't want to make a big thing of it, saying it out loud in front of the rest of the girls.

'What are you talking about?' Sarah replied. 'It's fine, don't worry about it.'

I didn't really mention it again, but after that, the two of us started to communicate more and got closer. As it turned out, we actually had stuff in common. I was always interested in cooking, and so was Sarah. She was always whipping up something in her flat, and she was good at it. It was simple things like that on which we found common ground. Eventually, we started going out together, and when we were working, we'd try to find fun things to do during the day. Nights out together became a regular thing, but there was often a point in the evening when I thought it was time to go home and Sarah did not. It might have been three or four in the morning, but when I'd suggest it was home time, Sarah would always give the same answer.

'No, I want to stay out!'

She was the party girl of the band, that was for sure. As much as I enjoyed a night out, I simply couldn't keep up with Sarah's pace, and I suppose that's when she started to make other friends who were more in tune with the hours she kept. People who shared her incredible level of energy!

Before long, Sarah had this whole new crowd of friends and was into a new scene, separate from what was going on within Girls Aloud. She was out clubbing, at bars, after-parties and house parties, and generally having a fine old time. None of us in the band were from London, so at the time, we didn't really have friends outside the band. Sarah, I suppose, was the first of us to break out of that, making her own friends outside the group. She was a social butterfly, with a tremendous amount of energy. Looking back, I think she felt like she belonged. People were always calling her, saying, 'let's do this or let's do that,' and I think there was something very intoxicating in that for Sarah. She didn't feel like she belonged in the band, and hadn't felt like she belonged at home in Manchester. Now here she was amid this crowd of fabulous people, a hugely famous pop star, having the time of her life. There was something so alive about her in those situations.

Consequently, people were queuing up to be her friend or even just to hang out or take pictures with her. It was the start of a whole new era for Sarah. Gone was the girl who was defrosting chickens on a Friday night so she could do a roast on Sunday. Here was Sarah Harding, the party girl. From then on, that was the perception of her. I was fortunate enough to have seen the other side of her, too.

When it was time to take a holiday, one of us suggested we should take a holiday together with our mums, and we both booked a holiday to Egypt. Although we booked them separately, we used the same travel agent and booked the same dates and flights. The night before we left for Egypt, my mum and I stayed at Sarah's mum's house in Manchester, as we were flying from Manchester airport. The next morning, we excitedly left for the airport – four gals taking on Egypt!

Only there was a small problem: when we arrived in Egypt, we realised that we were booked to go to completely different places. While Mum and I were booked into a beautiful hotel on the River Nile, Sarah and her mum were booked on a trip that included a dodgy-looking cruise up and down the Nile. They were even warned not to eat or drink anything. We were literally on two completely separate holidays and only met up again at the airport on the journey home. It was pretty awful. While Mum and I had enjoyed a lovely relaxing time, Sarah had ended up getting a parasite in her stomach, and she and her mum were totally stressed out.

From then on, Girls Aloud were in a whirl of single and album releases, recording, tours, roadshows, videos and photoshoots. Sarah was still full of energy. Even after the longest of days and most tiring of schedules, when we got back to London from wherever we'd been, Sarah would often put on a full face of make-up and get changed into a fresh outfit before heading off out into the night to some club or party.

I couldn't imagine going out dancing after the long hours we sometimes worked, but that was Sarah's world, and she enjoyed it. To be honest, that never really changed throughout the band, and she became famous for it. I remember being in LA and seeing a picture of Sarah in the American press. She had on a black dress, wore bright blonde hair, cut really short, and she was drinking from a bottle of Jack Daniels. I think that picture went around the world. I remember thinking, God, check out Sarah – she looks such a rock star!

I was happy that she was out having fun, but at the same time, I worried about her. I could see that some of the people she was hanging out with were definitely not looking out for her in the way real friends should. I felt some of them were only there for a seat at the best tables, the free drinks, the free rides and hotel rooms. Whenever it was, some of them were there because they wanted a piece of her celebrity, rather than her true friendship.

Sarah is a lovely, open and generous person, and she wants to connect with people. Sarah wanted to be loved, and she wanted to be heard. Unfortunately, there are certain types of people who will always take advantage of that generosity and openness. I think the eventual realisation of that took its toll on her emotionally. She got hurt by people who took advantage. There was this perception of Sarah that she was this rock-chick party girl, having the best time, but that wasn't always the case. Sometimes, I felt like that was the persona she thought she needed, just to fit in. Maybe the real Sarah was the fresh-faced girl with no make-up on, curled up, reading a book.

Sarah came alive on stage – and absolutely loved rocking out for all she was worth. She was brilliant in a live situation and very reliable. Like Sarah, I wasn't as accomplished a dancer as some of the other girls, so Sarah and I liked to make up for it in the live vocal side of things, particularly with ad-libs and harmonies. We had some great moments of singing and harmonising together, adding stuff that wasn't always on the recorded versions of the songs, but that added colour at the live shows. I recall one live concert video where you can still hear the two of us ad-libbing as we ran off the stage at the end of the show.

The downside was, she was always so stressed out and tense in the run-up to the show. In that respect, nothing had really changed since her days on *Popstars: The Rivals*. She worried so much that something wasn't going to work out or that she was going to mess up, that she often did mess up during rehearsals and then she'd be furious with herself. On the night, of course, she'd just blow everybody away.

When the time came to stand up and be counted, Sarah delivered every time. I got used to the fact that, although she tortured herself all the way through the process, it would be all right in the end.

Sarah loves to talk. She always has. For one work trip, we flew to New Zealand, and our travel time was 33 hours. Sarah and I sat together on the plane and, I kid you not, she talked for all of that 33 hours. I mean, the whole time. On the duration of that journey, we drank, we got sober, we drank again, and Sarah just talked throughout. I got the inside-out story of whatever guy she was seeing at the time – this part, that part, what did happen, what didn't and what might happen.

When we got to New Zealand, it was all grand and off we went to work. While on the trip, I met a guy who I really liked in Australia, but with our schedules as mad as they were, I didn't really get time to fill Sarah in on all the gossip or even tell her about this guy. So, on the way home, as Sarah and I settled into our seats together, I felt like it was a good time to tell Sarah what had been going on with me.

I literally got about half a sentence out when Sarah said, 'Yeah, babe, sorry. I'm tired. I'm just going to go to sleep.'

'YOU'RE WHAT?' My voice went up about three octaves. 'I listened to you going on for thirty-three hours non-stop on the way here, and now you want to go to sleep!'

'I don't remember that,' she said, genuinely oblivious.

Over the years, I've tried to be there for Sarah in the way a big sister would, even though I'm younger than she is. Knowing she's quite vulnerable and hates confrontation, I have tried, on occasion, to step in when I felt like someone was taking advantage of her or speaking inappropriately to her. I hated the idea that some people thought they could talk to Sarah in a way they wouldn't talk to anybody else. Whether it was someone we worked with in a live situation, or in the studio, or one of our team, talking down to her as if she were stupid or a naughty child. I don't think it's because many of them were terrible people; it's more that some people around us saw her as an easy target, perhaps because she always seemed so eager to please. I saw it happen a lot, and it upset me. Nobody would have spoken to me like that, so why were they doing it to Sarah?

We all got together recently, all five of Girls Aloud – I'm sure Sarah is going to tell you all about it at some point in the book. Given Sarah's circumstances, it was a really wonderful thing, us all being together, but I felt like my eyes might fill with tears every time she spoke. Why? Because it was the first time I could ever remember that Sarah was the main focus of attention, just chatting away normally. No drama. She was just telling us all where she went for dinner or what she bought at the supermarket. We were all listening to her. We were all focused on her. For the first time ever, Sarah was given the floor.

The whole experience was a reminder of just how funny and open she is and how she really doesn't care. Whatever life throws at her, she'll go about her business and remain essentially Sarah. There was a lot of laughter and honesty, and I found the whole experience very moving. It was probably one of the few times everybody got to see Sarah as she really is. As sad as I felt for what she was going through, I was, in that respect, really happy for her.

CHAPTER NINE

When I think about it, a lot of the stories I have about Girls Aloud shenanigans seem to involve Nadine and me. On one occasion, early on in our career, I almost missed a crucial moment, not once but twice.

We'd all flown out to Los Angeles to record some songs with Brian Higgins, who had a house up in the hills at the time. I remember us all being ridiculously excited because we were flying business class, which was a first for all of us. Nadine and I fell utterly in love with LA, and the minute we had some time off, we went like proper tourists. We went to Venice Beach and ate candy floss, and I bought a Santa Monica hoodie, which I still have. At the end of the trip, we had some time off, so Nadine suggested we fly to Vegas together as she was going to stay with her dad out there. I was still with Mikey at the time, so I asked if he'd like to come out to Vegas and join me if I bought him a flight. It felt nice finally being in a position where I could do stuff like that, and I knew we'd have a great time together. I've always liked to treat friends, especially my mates who weren't lucky enough to be able to afford to do some of the things I did. If I wanted to share time with someone, I was happy to pick up the bill so we could be together. I have to say, over the years, some people have been less appreciative than others, but that's another story!

The problem with Mikey making such a short trip out to Vegas was the eight-hour time difference. He was so jet-lagged during his three-day stay, I think he ended up sleeping for most of the time he was there. I ended up wandering around some of the casinos on my own. I'm not really a gambler, but I did enjoy myself playing the slot machines.

On the way back, Nadine was due to fly on the same flight from LAX as Mikey and me, but it was cancelled. We were told that there were two other flights we might be able to get on. Some-how, we got separated, and while Nadine was able to get on the first available flight, Mikey and I were not. It was frustrating and nerve-wracking too, as we were due to appear at the TMF Awards in the Netherlands two days later. TMF was a Dutch music channel and Girls Aloud had been nominated for an award, and we were also performing, so it was quite a big deal for us. There was worse to come, however. Our second flight was also cancelled, so the next thing I knew, we were on a bloody shuttle bus being shipped to a hotel overnight as there were no more flights to London. By this time, I was out of my mind, knowing that I was supposed to get back to London, get my shit together at home, and then get on a flight to Holland for the awards. As time went on, I realised that just wasn't going to happen, so I started looking at how I could fly straight from LA to Holland. I got so overwrought about the idea of letting the girls down and missing the awards, I was a mess.

I can still see myself, screaming and crying on the phone in LAX with Mikey by my side.

'Will you just please try to calm down?' he was saying. 'It's all going to be fine.'

I couldn't calm down, though. I was worried about getting into trouble for being a no-show. Even if I did fly straight to Holland, how was I going to get my dress and all my stuff for the ceremony?

In the end, Mikey ended up flying back to London while I had to take a separate flight. Never mind that I'd originally had my first-ever business class ticket; I was now stuck at the rear of the plane and had to lump it. There I was, squashed in economy, crying and rocking all the way to Holland.

To make matters worse, I got stopped and searched at the airport, which held me up further, and I knew that the soundcheck for our performance was imminent. Honestly, by that point, it had been over 24 hours of absolute high-stress, and my nerves were in shreds.

I finally made it to the soundcheck by the skin of my teeth. Luckily, our tour manager, Drew, had managed to pack a spare black dress for me to wear, so at least that was sorted. The only problem was, there was only one pair of heels going spare, which belonged to Cheryl. Yes, Cheryl, who is a size 3, while I'm a size 5. We did our performance of 'Love Machine', with me tottering around in silver shoes which were two sizes too small for me, but even then my drama wasn't over. Later, as we sat in the audience waiting for the announcement of the winner of the Best UK Act, I was suddenly desperate for a pee. I asked if I could go several times, but Drew kept telling me that I had to wait for a break, just in case.

When the show finally went to a break, I darted out to the loo with Drew escorting me. There I was, sitting on the toilet mid-flow when suddenly I hear, 'And the winners are ... Girls Aloud!'

'OH MY FUCKING GOD!' I'd endured the whole nightmarish trip from America to Holland, fuelled by nervous energy and sheer force of will, and I'd still somehow managed to miss our award announcement.

Poor Drew, who'd been lurking outside the ladies' loo, shouted from behind the door, 'Sarah! Get off the bloody toilet!'

I had to stop myself mid-wee, pull up my knickers and run. Drew all but threw me up the stairs from the toilets and back down them into the auditorium.

'Tell the girls to walk slowly,' he shouted at someone.

We had to cross over a walkway to get to the stage, and while the girls strolled on demurely, there was little old me, tearing along behind them to catch up. It looked like I was excited to receive our award, but in truth I was just rushing to catch the girls up to get to the stage in time. When we got up there, I grabbed the award and yelled, 'YES!'

When you have the reputation of being the crazy, scatty one, sometimes people can think the worst of you even when you're entirely innocent. In 2006, the Mayor of London, Ken Livingstone, invited us to Shanghai to perform, showing communist China a bit of what UK pop music had to offer. It was a cultural trip regarding trade relations between London and Shanghai, as the mayor's office also had an office there. Unfortunately, we arrived amid a bloody monsoon, so it wasn't the best weather to experience the city. Still, Nadine and I got out there and saw the sights, visiting a temple while we had the chance – all with a camera crew in tow as we were filming our documentary TV show, *Off the Record*, at the time for Channel 4. The other girls weren't quite as mad keen as we were, so holed up in the hotel for the day.

The reception itself, where we were performing, was a huge deal. We were doing a scaled-down version of our set, but it wasn't our finest performance by any stretch of the imagination. The mayor looked like he was enjoying himself, but I think some of our sexy moves might have been a bit risqué for that particular audience.

The funniest part of that trip happened behind the scenes. The girls were often playing pranks, and Hillary was often on the receiving end. Now, I am going to state my case here and tell you that I was not a prank player, and did not take part in any practical jokes, although on one occasion the girls decided to use me as bait.

They anonymously rang one of the assistants working on the event. I'm not sure exactly which of the girls it was, but they told the assistant that one of Girls Aloud was inebriated and lying semi-naked outside one of the lifts on their floor of the hotel. Of course, the assistant called Hillary immediately, as the girls knew they would. The assistant explained to Hillary that, as the band member was partially clothed and in a state, they couldn't approach or touch her in any way for fear of accusations or reprisals. They suggested that Hills sort out the situation herself, and get her band member safely to bed. On hearing this, Hillary's immediate reaction was, 'Oh my God! Sarah!'

Never mind the fact that nobody had mentioned any name whatsoever. Hills just assumed it must be me, exactly as the girls knew she would.

The next day at breakfast, I greeted Hillary with a good morning, noticing that she didn't look all that happy. I was with Nicola having breakfast at the time.

'Are you OK, Hills? I asked, bright-eyed and ready for the day.

To be honest, I was the only one who *was* bright-eyed, as I'd not stayed up drinking with the rest of the girls.

'Fine,' Hillary said, but she certainly didn't look it. 'I can take a joke like the rest of you.'

Nicola leant across the table. 'You'll never guess what we did to Hillary last night. We told her you were passed out naked outside a lift, so she came to find you.'

It turned out that when Hills had gone out to rescue me and save my dignity, the girls had been hiding around the corner when Hills came down from her floor to ours. They'd heard the ding of the lift and then Hillary's voice – quiet at first, then gradually getting louder: 'Sarah! Sarah!'

Of course, she was wandering around the hotel corridor looking for me, not realising that I was safely tucked up in bed because I was so jet-lagged. I could just imagine it. They were so bad those girls, particularly Nicola, Kimberley and Cheryl. Nadine got involved in the pranks sometimes, but I never did.

On another occasion – I can't remember where – they told Hillary that the police were outside a hotel and that Nadine was going to be arrested for not paying her taxes. I'd never seen Drew move so fast, trying to sneak us out of the back entrance of a hotel. The long and the short of the story is that I'm often seen as the troublemaker of the band. I think not! They were sneaky little buggers sometimes, those girls!

It was quite an honour to be asked to perform at an event like the one in Shanghai. Those were the moments I learned to appreciate being in Girls Aloud. Those wonderful and unique things I got to do, and the fantastic people I got to meet.

I've met so many famous people over the years, some real superstars. I have so much respect for people like that: people who have worked hard to get where they are in such a tough business. I've not actually met my biggest idols – well, not properly – but then again, that's probably a good thing, right? They say never meet your heroes in case they don't live up to your expectations in real life. That's definitely a bubble I wouldn't want to burst.

I suppose my idols are all similar in some ways. They're all strong, talented women, all musicians, all big stars. Growing up, it was Madonna. I loved her image, her music, her strength and attitude and the ways she pushed boundaries in so many areas. Still, I think she might be intimidating in person. Another of my idols is Lady Gaga. I actually did kind of meet her, when I was backstage at *The X Factor* one time. Gaga was in a dressing room next door to us, and as she was on our label, Claire Close, our TV promoter at Polydor, was looking after her. I wish I'd have gotten the chance for a proper introduction, but it didn't happen.

Gwen Stefani has always been a massive influence for me too. I remember in the early days when our Polydor MD, Colin Barlow, had called me into his office to talk. He knew I'd been unhappy at the start of the band, wanting to write more and sing more, and he tried to assure me how important my role in the band was. He told me I could be an icon within the band if I put my mind to it. While I was with him, he was playing a track for me to get my opinion. It was almost as if he wanted to get a feel for my musical ear. At one point, Colin asked me to listen to the song they were planning to be Gwen Stefani's next release. The song was 'What You Waiting For?'. Colin asked me what I thought of it, and I told him it was a smash! Thinking back, maybe I should have tried my luck working in A&R – I'd have been good at that. I always had an ear for what would be a hit.

Sometime later, in 2004, we did our first *Royal Variety Performance*. We performed our single 'The Show', starting the performance sitting under old-fashioned hairdryers. We wore outfits that look a bit like glamorous, tight-fitting hairdresser's tabards, in black and pink. During the instrumental break of the song, we all disappeared behind curtains, only to be revealed again in fabulously co-ordinated red dresses. Gwen was on the same bill as us that year, and I remember thinking how fantastic she looked when I saw her backstage after the show. I asked her who her shoes were by, and told her how much I wanted them. I was so into Gwen's music – it was smart, slick pop, just like Madonna before her and Gaga after. In fact, I've always seen Gaga as a bit of a cross between Gwen Stefani and Madonna – in all the best ways. All three of them could be both tough and sweet when they wanted to be, and that was something I both loved and admired.

I did have one very starstruck moment, while I was out at Nobu Malibu with Stephen Dorff. Cher was sitting on the table right next to us. I'd been a huge fan of hers growing up. The funny thing about that was, Cher is Calum Best's godmother, although I never met her while I was dating him. Cher had become great friends with Calum's mum, Angie, when she accompanied Cher on tour as her fitness instructor, back in the day. I do remember how on that occasion I was silently screaming inside with excitement.

During the time I've been working on this chapter, I've unexpectedly ended up back in the hospital. Mum wanted them to look me over and keep an eye on me because I've had a couple of incidents where I've fallen over. Also Mum says I seem a bit confused sometimes. Last week, when I fell down, I couldn't get up. Then, there was another time when I was trying to get a sweater over my head. I felt weak, and it was a struggle, and in the end I felt like I couldn't breathe, which brought on a panic attack. Mum had to come running in to help me. She stood by me and told me to breathe … breathe … until I'd calmed down and it had subsided. It's strange how something that would typically be so simple becomes such a mammoth undertaking when you're sick. It's a new normal that I'm not sure I'll ever get used to.

To be honest, I think Mum needs the respite as much as I do, and I really need it. I guess what's called for is some special-ised medical care, and that's what I'll get here at The Christie.

This week, I started my sessions of radiotherapy, so it's like one thing on top of another. The radiotherapy leaves me tired, confused and weak most of the time. It wipes me out. It's no wonder I've been a bit unsteady on my feet. I'd been told that radiotherapy isn't generally as invasive as the chemo, but, quite honestly, the way I've been feeling after the first couple of sessions, I'll take the chemo any day.

It's never a dull moment in hospital. They start their rounds at six, and from then on it feels like someone or other is coming in to do something every ten minutes: take blood, do my vitals, change my cannula, deliver a menu and take my order for lunch – today it's tuna and cucumber with soda bread. Nice.

Once again, I'm just so impressed and moved at the hard work of the caregivers in this place. They don't stop.

Today I've got a full schedule. Various appointments and tests, but with my head all over the place like it is, I can't always remember what they are. I do know I have an MRI booked in, and I think that's the big event of the day. Fingers crossed the findings are positive.

While I've been sitting here in my hospital bed, Cheryl has WhatsApped me to see how I am. The girls have all been so supportive throughout this. It's a really lovely feeling to know that they're all thinking about me, and it's great for us to finally be reconnecting.

CHAPTER TEN

For a while in 2006, I dated the actor Stephen Dorff, but the way that all came about was quite strange. It all started while Stephen was over filming in the UK. He'd seen me on the front of *Arena* magazine with the girls and decided he liked the look of me. It really was one of those 'his people called my people' situations. Not the way you'd expect a romance to start out, and it almost didn't happen at all. Stephen had asked one of his assistants to get my number, so Angela from our management team called to tell me while my mum and I were getting our nails done in a salon in Hampstead.

'Stephen Dorff has asked for your number,' Angela said. 'What should I tell his assistant?'

I was a bit miffed, to be honest. 'If he thinks I'm just dishing out my number to someone I don't even know, Angela, he's got another think coming,' I said. 'That's not the way it works with me. If he wants to get in touch with me, tell his PA to send us his number. Then maybe I'll call.'

As it turned out, Stephen did send his phone number over, but once I'd got it I felt timid about calling him, after all my bravado, so I just left it for a while. Maybe I should just have let him call me after all. By the time I finally plucked up the courage to call him, he was in the airport lounge at Heathrow, ready to fly back to LA. I was a bit gutted to tell you the truth.

The funny thing was, we got on quite well on that first call, and so we ended up staying in touch. In fact, we spoke quite often. It got to the stage, over the next few months, when we were literally talking every night … and for hours on end. Sometimes, we'd be on the phone chatting until the early hours. Well, it was the early hours for me; he was in Los Angeles, eight hours behind UK time. When he called me in the evening, it was two or three in the morning for me, so I'd invariably end up feeling exhausted during the day for weeks and weeks on end. I mean, I was hanging up with Stephen at 4am and then getting up to rehearse for our Chemistry tour, singing and dancing for hours at a time. I've already mentioned how much concentration I had to give when it came to choreography, so you can just imagine. That was mentally draining enough, without being up half the night for all that transatlantic canoodling!

As tired as I was, the calls were quite romantic. Stephen had a lovely way about him and was always so sweet to me. Sometimes, he would even play the piano for me, which he did really well. He could sing well too. Like me, he'd never had any formal musical training, but he learned a lot from his father Steve Dorff (Sr), who is a well-known country music songwriter and producer.

After many nights of talking for hours, there was something between us, even though we'd never even met. I think we were slowly falling in love with one another's personalities, and that felt kind of nice after all the drama of Mikey and Calum. The nightly phones worked for me in another way in that they were something of a routine; something regular. At the time, that was good for me. By this time, we were on tour, and there was always the option to go out and get crazy. Having my routine, late-night calls with Stephen kept me on a good, steady level. Although I was absolutely knackered all the time, I couldn't wait to meet him.

That meeting was to be right before the final night of our Chemistry tour, on 3 June 2006, at the newly renovated Wembley Arena. It was in the midst of such an exciting time. Our first tour, What Will the Neighbours Say?, had been in concert halls and playhouses up and down the country, but here we were, playing arenas of 10,000-plus people.

The day before the last show, I had a day off, so I went to meet him at his hotel: Blakes in Kensington. Of course, I was apprehensive. I mean, talking to someone is one thing, but an in-the-flesh meeting with a handsome Hollywood movie star is enough to make even the coolest girl's heart beat a little faster. Plus, it was all so shrouded in secrecy, I remember feeling like I was going to meet James Bond! It's funny, the first thing I thought when we met face-to-face was that he was shorter than I'd imagined, about five foot seven, but certainly very good-looking with a sexy smile – no complaints there. Anyway, what difference did a couple of inches matter when I'd already fallen for his personality.

We chatted in the bar for quite some time after I got there. It felt weird putting a real face to the voice after all that time. It had been four months of over-the-phone courtship, and he hadn't got bored and given up. For that, I had to give him kudos. Stephen was no disappointment either, and I have to admit the whole thing felt quite seductive. Electrifying even. I felt like we'd known one another for ages, and in a funny way, I suppose we had.

I won't go into all the details of the evening – a girl's got to retain some mystery – but I did end up staying the night with him at Blakes.

The next night, Stephen came to Wembley to see us on the final night of the tour. Later, he came along to the after-party at a club in London – which for the life of me I can't remember the name of … chemo brain! Anyway, it was a great do; food and drink were flowing and a good time was had by all. Of course, there were so many people I had to thank and chat to at the party, I hardly got to see Stephen. He spent half the party looking for me. Unfortunately, and, some might say typically, I'd had one too many shots. So on top of all that food and a bit of dancing, I had to dash to the toilet to throw up. I remember hiding out there for a while until I felt better and was ready to face the party guests again – not to mention Stephen. Eventually, he found me just as I was emerging, refreshed and ready for round two. Luckily, I had some mints at the time.

After that, we circled the party together, chatting with various people and having some more drinks. It was the thing when I was younger. You got sick after consuming too much alcohol, but then carried on drinking afterwards. Throw up and carry on! Not something I could ever do now.

Anyway, at the end of the party Stephen and I somehow ended up back at Blakes together, but that night I just had a shower and we went to bed. There was no rumpy-pumpy of any description.

A few weeks later, I was supposed to fly to New York to see him, but it all went tits up. I was shopping in Selfridges when I got a call to say that his plans had changed.

Eventually, I planned a three-week trip to LA, so we planned to be together for that. I'd organised some meetings and songwriting sessions out there, and the plan was that I would use Stephen's place as a base for the duration of my trip. Unfortunately, my extended stay seemed to freak him the fuck out; I remember his assistant telling me that he'd never had a girlfriend stay for more than a couple of nights, and here I was staying for three weeks.

It wasn't like I was expecting him to be glued to me the whole time either. The idea was that I'd do my thing and he would do his. Girls Aloud were signed to EMI Music Publishing, so I had some meetings with a guy called Ed from the LA branch of our publishers, while Stephen was doing whatever he had to do.

I realised things weren't as they should be when, on a couple of occasions, he went out for meetings and then disappeared. He'd call to tell me he was on his way back, so I could get ready, and we could go out for a bite, but it would end with me all dressed up with nowhere to go. Stephen, meanwhile, had gone somewhere else, and then somewhere else after that.

When we were together, Stephen was quieter than he'd been during our months of late-night phone calls. He liked to read or sit outside on the beautiful terrace of his house on Malibu Beach.

It was clear that he felt uncomfortable with me being there, and I felt uneasy being there, too. One morning, I had breakfast with one of his PAs and I told her how I felt.

'I guess he can be a bit of a brat when he wants to be,' she said. 'It's just the way it is with him sometimes. I guess you either put up with it or you don't.'

'You know what, babe?' I said. 'I don't think I will. Do you think you could find me a room at the Viceroy in Santa Monica?'

I ended up at the Viceroy and had some more meetings with Ed, who agreed to set me up with some great co-writers. I remember suddenly feeling alone while I was staying at the hotel, with not much to do. At the time, Nadine was going out with *Desperate Housewives* actor Jesse Metcalfe, so she was over in LA with him. We hung out a couple of times at the Sky Bar, but at the time they were hard to pin down, so our plans didn't always work out. There were times in between my writing sessions that I was at such a loss at what to do, with no real friends in the city; I remember driving to The Beverly Centre a few times to visit the pet store just so I could hang out with the puppies.

Eventually Ed set me up a meeting with Diane Warren, who'd written songs for Celine Dion, Whitney Houston, Lady Gaga, Cher and Beyoncé to name a tiny few. It was so great meeting with her; she was lovely, and I had so much admiration for everything she'd done. Diane actually reminded me of Chrissie Hynde, whose song 'I'll Stand By You' had given Girls Aloud their second number one in 2004. Diane had listened to some Girls Aloud tracks but said she wished she could have heard my voice more in among the girls. At the time, that made me feel a bit sad. I guess that was before I'd really had my chance to shine vocally within the band.

While I was at the Viceroy, I got the most hideous food poisoning and had to miss some of my co-writing sessions. I started to feel like the entire trip had been a bit of a disaster. First, there'd been the whole thing with Stephen and now this. After my meetings with Ed, I really thought this could be the start of something great – a chance to write songs with teams who were writing for artists like Tina Turner and also an emerging artist called Robin Thicke – but something as stupid as a few mouthfuls of dodgy food had thrown it all up in the air. I was acutely aware that my potential co-writers would think that I wasn't committed. If I couldn't commit a first time, they weren't going to bother giving me a second chance. I was bummed out to say the least.

It wasn't long before I was due to leave to come home, so I somehow pulled myself together and forced myself out of the hotel to my last few co-writing sessions. I did see Stephen again, too. He came out and met me with Nadine, and called to ask if I wanted to go out for a bite to eat. There was no real animosity, but when he didn't turn up to meet me one day, I just stopped believing in him. He obviously had other priorities now, which I found strange because, for all those months, his priority had been to call me every night for hours on end. It rang in my head what the people who worked for him had told me – that they had seen him behave this way before. It wasn't just me, so that was that.

CHAPTER
ELEVEN

While I was in hospital last week, I had some news that really hit hard. I'm not sure I've even really processed it yet. I'm not even sure how a person can process that kind of news.

An MRI scan revealed that I have another tumour, either at the base of my spine or on my brain. I knew something was up. It felt like I'd been wearing a hat that was too tight for too long. One scan revealed lesions between my hair and my skin that were swollen. An MRI revealed another tumour, which means that the spread of the disease has worsened, as had my prognosis. This tumour is the thing that scares me more than anything because I think it will be the thing that affects me the most.

I don't know what it's going to do, but it's there. There was an option for radiotherapy on my skull but I don't want to go through that and lose my hair at this stage, especially with no guarantees at the end of it.

'At the end of the day, we're fighting multiple different areas now,' I told the doctors. 'We've got a new chemotherapy plan, so I'd rather stick to that.'

It might seem vain thinking about my hair, but my thinking was that if there's a chance I've only got six months, then I've got six months. Losing my hair probably wasn't going to change that, so if there's another way to manage the disease or treat it, then let's do that. I don't want to feel like I have to spend whatever time I have left hiding away.

My new regimen of treatment includes this oral chemotherapy, where I take ten pills a day. So now I'm having a dose of chemo, then two weeks of pills, then a week's break. After that, it all starts over again. At the moment, it's a new thing so I feel like I'm sitting here waiting for whatever side effects might come, although I have no idea what they might be. All I know is that my body aches like absolute hell: my neck, my back, my chest.

The way things are going, I'm going to end up with a Stannah stair lift and a walking frame, shouting at kids in the street like a very pissed-off old woman.

OK, so I'm not exactly there yet, but, I'm not going to lie, I do feel like I'm missing a lot of life.

It's very hard thinking about it and talking about it, so my plan is to just crack on. I want to get this book done, and doing it gives me something else to focus on rather than pain, medication and chemo.

n 2006, the band agreed to participate in the *Most Haunted* spin-off show, *Ghosthunting with … Girls Aloud*. Well, I say the band;

in the end only four of us ended up doing it, as poor Nadine was too scared. This was the first-ever episode of the show, with Nicola, Cheryl, Kimberley and me looking for ghosts in two separate places in North Wales. One of them was Plas Teg, which is a Grade I listed Jacobean house, said to be one of the most haunted houses in Wales.

Yvette Fielding, the primary host of the show, took us around the place where there were all sorts of weird banging and noises and spooky goings-on. Going in there, I was billy-big-bollocks, confident that everything that happened was going to be a set-up, designed to scare the crap out of us. I'd watched all the *Most Haunted* shows and loved them, so I was really quite into it, but I knew a lot of it was just scary fun. I have to admit, there was a definite shift in my attitude as the show went on, and I started to feel like there really was something to it all. At a certain point, my voice very clearly went from ultra-cocky to 'please don't hurt us'. Some of the other girls were just as bad. I remember Nicola was quite scared. She'd been relatively quiet for a while until her heavy Liverpudlian accent rang out in the darkness.

'What the fuck was that?' And, 'Get me the fuck out of here!'

I love all the girls' varied accents, and I'm pretty spot on with the impersonations. Nadine's is probably the hardest – that strong Northern Irish twang. If I'm relaxed and have had a couple of drinks, I can usually get it down pat.

During a seance, objects were being thrown around the room. It was supposedly the presence of some squire who used to work there and who didn't like women. At one point something went flying past my ear, there was a bang, and I screamed. After that, I was a complete wreck, and all my bravado disappeared, especially after the loud bang that made us all scream and run out. It's pretty hilarious to watch back. There was one funny moment in another room where Cheryl said, 'If you're here, just tap the fucking table!' It tapped, loudly, and I swear there was nobody in that room but us. After another fast, screaming exit, I turned to Cheryl in the darkness.

'Cheryl! What the fuck did you do that for?'

The other place we went on *Ghosthunting* was Crossley Hospital, which was an old tuberculosis sanatorium in Cheshire. It was virtually derelict, but there was a morgue and another part of the building where the nurses used to live. Again, Nicola eventually bailed on the group, but I followed suit pretty soon afterwards. Ultimately, I gathered my nerve to rejoin Cheryl and Kimberley again, but when somebody started throwing stones at us in the basement of the building, we all decided that enough was enough. We all headed for the safety of the taxi, while Yvette stayed on to face the evil spirit. It was terrifying at the time, but actually one of my favourite things we did on TV. I loved it.

In 2008 we made a TV series called *The Passions of Girls Aloud* for ITV2. The premise of the show was that each one of us had an episode demonstrating something we were passionate about other than singing. Nicola's was creating a make-up range, Cheryl's was street dancing, Kimberley tried out in a West End musical, and I was to play in a polo tournament, training in the UK and in Argentina. Nadine was supposed to be conducting an orchestra, but I don't think she'd ever been all that keen on the idea of doing the show, so it didn't end up happening. She was always the most reserved as far as that kind of stuff went.

For me, *Passions* turned out to be an experience that was painful but fun. It was pretty brutal, and I now have a tremendous amount of respect for polo players. One of the things I'm proudest of is that I'm such an all-rounder. I'm always up for trying something new, however out of my comfort zone it might be. Despite my love for and experience of horses, this was on another level altogether. Still, I felt up to the challenge.

Polo is played with two teams, and the aim is to score goals using a long wooden mallet to hit a small ball through the other team's goal. Each team has four horses with riders, and the game is divided into sections called chukkas. It's a contact sport where you can be moving at up to 30 miles an hour while people are trying to hook your stick and ride into you. It's certainly no walk in the park.

I trained in England first and then in Buenos Aires, Argentina, which was fantastic. I started very early each day – which as you can imagine wasn't easy for me – and ended the day knackered but feeling rewarded.

The first horse they put me on was called Pablo, and he was just amazing. For me, he was the perfect horse, and we quickly developed a bond and a rhythm. I was sad to leave him, but when a monsoon flooded the pitch in Buenos Aires, we had to film the final of the tournament in Hickstead in West Sussex. That was a bit of a shock to me. It was an arena, rather than a field, which wasn't what I'd been accustomed to. This meant that there was a lot more turning involved, rather than straight galloping – which is what I was good at. I was in a small arena using a bigger ball on sand rather than grass. I felt so unsteady. I'd also never ridden on three of the four ponies I was given on the day. In fact, I'd only practised on one of them for a while the day before.

I'd have loved to have kept the same pony throughout, the one I'd had a bit of experience riding, but that was impossible. You have to change the horse at each chukka as they get tired. The horses are galloping up and down fields the size of three football pitches.

Cheryl and Kimberley came to watch me play in the final, and it was pretty brutal. I'll admit that I was entirely out of my depth that day. If it had been in the open space of a field, I might have just struggled through, but being in a small arena with all that twisting and turning was simply too much. I didn't have the skills required, so I kept losing my grip. At one point, I lost a stirrup and almost slipped off. Luckily, my friend Jamie Morrison, who was in the other team, helped me back on and I continued. It happened again, though, and this time my horse was determined to follow the ball, which was in a scrum. I'd lost my stirrup and I felt myself slipping off, but I was terrified of being in a crush, as that can be deadly. Jamie's father had ended up in a coma from which he never woke from being caught in a crush during polo. My brother had also had friends who had died or been injured. Realising there wasn't much else I could do, I let myself fall, knocking myself out when I hit the ground. I lay there looking like the chalked-out shape of a dead body. It was funny but not funny. I was only out for about 30 seconds, but the worst part of the injury was to my ankle. When I first came to, I didn't have a clue where I was or what had happened. It was the weirdest feeling in the world, and it scared me. In fact, I was in tears.

Of course, with this being reality TV, the cameras were on me. My brother came over and told them to 'get lost'.

'This is serious; she needs to be checked over,' he said.

In the end, I shook it off, but the organisers advised that I shouldn't carry on. As it turned out, my team won anyway, so they let me keep the trophy!

The experience certainly didn't put me off riding. It's something I continued to enjoy, although the idea of being on a horse right now seems like another universe away.

CHAPTER
TWELVE

've always been able to adapt to whatever group of people or the environment I've been in. I think that life skill stems from a couple of things. Firstly, it comes from the number of different settings I was in as a child and a young person: the various schools, the multiple jobs. I encountered so many varied types of people and situations, and I learned to fit in and go with the flow of whatever was going on around me. As I got older, I felt like I was often playing a character to fit in, to the point where I sometimes didn't really know which one was the real me any more. It's something I probably wasn't aware of for much of the time, but I can certainly see it now. Still, there were upsides to this. It's actually convenient to be able to adapt to varied environments so quickly. I have friends who are quite posh – Lady Victoria Hervey and all the polo crowd, for instance. I've also got mates from the East End of London and Southend who are not at all posh – proper Essex, in fact. Then there are my other group of friends from Hampstead in London – a completely different crowd. I can enjoy my time with all of them in any kind of situations because I guess I know what they are expecting of me. I always have the perfect Sarah on tap to fit into their worlds.

Of course, I also have my on-stage persona. I sometimes think that's the Sarah I like best, because the place I feel most at home is on stage, performing. That's where I can let rip and feel free. I certainly stepped into a character while I was up there in front of a Girls Aloud audience, but that was for me as much as it was for an audience.

Our early gigs were great fun, particularly G-A-Y in London, where we'd always try to pull something special out of the bag. In the beginning, when we weren't big enough to tour, G-A-Y was a brilliant opportunity for us to put on a show. We always spent every penny we were paid on the show itself. On one Saturday at G-A-Y, the theme of the night was 'school disco', so we dressed up as school girls – oh my God, imagine that now! We came on stage to 'We don't need no education' from 'Another Brick in the Wall' by Pink Floyd, who Dad and I are both big fans of. On another night it was a pyjama party, and when the curtain went up, we were all in beds, with naked men under the covers. I think a lot of the G-A-Y audience probably appreciated that one.

Of all the tours we did down the line, Tangled Up in 2008 was definitely my favourite. We started the show flying above the stage with billowing wing-like capes, and I had this crazy curly hair. I think most people know that on stage I was always 'extra'. I remember at the start of one show I shouted, 'Big Mouth's back, and she's here to say hello!'

One of the songs from that tour was 'Girl Overboard', which was from the *Tangled Up* album. It was a fantastic track, and the Girls Aloud single that never was. I had a sneaking suspicion the song was written about me. However, it was apparently written about a member of another girl band. This was a song I loved singing on tour, always adding in new harmonies. It was a real moment. Cheryl loved the song too and said it should have been a single. In the end, it was a toss-up with this and 'Can't Speak French', which is what won out in the end.

Going back further, on the Chemistry tour of 2006, we'd put together a movie medley, with eighties favourites 'Fame', 'Flash-dance (What a Feeling)' and 'Footloose'. My big number within the medley was, of course, 'Footloose', the rock-out number of the three. It was brilliant fun and went down so well with the fans that Polydor felt that we should record one of the songs for inclu-sion on our first greatest hits album, *The Sound of Girls Aloud*. The thing that not many people know is that we were initially going to do a Spice Girls medley on that tour, which we'd rehearsed and perfected, right up to the dress rehearsal. That's when the problem arose as the show was running too long. We had to get rid of some-thing. So, on the day of the first show, our Spice Girls medley got axed, but the movie medley made it in.

We ended up recording 'What a Feeling' for the greatest hits album, and some other new songs. One of these was 'Something Kinda Ooooh', which seemed to go through quite a lot of different versions at Xenomania before the final one we ended up with.

Around the time of 'Something Kinda Ooooh's release, we all bowled into Polydor for a meeting with Peter Loraine, now general manager of our label Fascination Records, and the MD, Colin Barlow. We were excited about releasing our first greatest hits compilation, which seemed like such a milestone, and whatever was to come next. At one point in the meeting, Nicola asked the question: 'So what's going to be our next single after "Something Kinda Ooooh"?'

'We think we're going to go with "What a Feeling",' Colin said, and suddenly all five of us hit the roof.

'No way are we having that as a single!' we shouted, practically in unison.

'I'm not singing the Gaviscon advert on telly!' Cheryl screamed.

We didn't even really want 'What a Feeling' to go on the album, let alone be a single. Cheryl had a last-minute idea of recording another eighties classic, 'I Think We're Alone Now'. This song had been a number one hit for Tiffany in 1987 but was actually an old sixties tune by Tommy James & the Shondells. Of course, we were all much more familiar with the Tiffany version. The only trouble with this idea was that the album was literally due to be pressed any day. Hence, the recording of it was an absolute rush job; the version of 'I Think We're Alone Now' that went on the album isn't as polished as the one that eventually came out as a single, in fact it doesn't even sound like it's finished. It's kind of ruined it for me really, as this had been one of my favourite songs as a child.

I was usually very up when we came off stage after a show. 'Let's go out!' would be my mantra, and often it would be me and the dancers, to whom I was always close, who would go out. We had some fantastic dancers over the years, including Simon Barnum, who's one of my best friends and continued to work with me as a choreographer once I'd left the band. Then there was Arthur Gourounlian, Anthony Kaye, Aaron Bernard, Craig Whymark, Jerry Reeve, Mark Webb – all under the supervision of our choreographer and creative director, Beth Honan.

We were lucky enough to have so many great people on our team over the years, both on tour and on our many photo shoots and videos: Liz Martins and Kolbrun Ran (make-up) and Lisa Laudat (hair) and of course my dear friend Sarah O'Brian AKA Mousey, were all on team 'glam squad' at various times. They certainly had their work cut out for them with the five of us, especially with all our varied tastes and styles.

For the 'Call the Shots' video, I thought I could get away with a sharp crop haircut, but I ended up looking a bit like Mr Spock. That was one I definitely regretted. If I'm being honest, I think that's a look that only gorgeous, skinny models can get away with. We all went to LA to film that video, but you wouldn't know it; it could have been anywhere.

There were also our stylists Victoria Adcock and Frank Strachan. Also, Toby Leighton Pope, who was our promoter, Sol Parker, who was our agent, and Jeremy Hewitt, our merchandiser. I affectionally named those boys The Three Stooges, and we had some great and funny times with them on our various tours. Some of which I probably shouldn't mention here!

While we were on tour in Ireland, we were all staying at the Dylan Hotel, which is a gorgeous boutique hotel in Dublin's south city centre. We'd been partying quite hard in the private outside area we'd been given. The music was pumping, and we were all singing, dancing and swinging around poles like pole dancers.

Eventually, the party was finished, but some of us were not, if you know what I mean. It wasn't unusual for a hardcore bunch of us to end up in one of the rooms where we'd carry on the party – music still going. God only knows what the other guests must have thought, but it was morning before anyone could find us. Apparently, Drew and the rest of the security team had no idea where I was and had been searching for hours. As you can imagine, they weren't best pleased. In fact, I remember one of them being quite cross with me when I was eventually located.

'Are you fuckin' packed, Sarah?' he shouted over.

'Yes, I'm packed,' I said.

I actually wasn't completely packed, but I didn't have much stuff, and it was all right there in my room. I just had to get to the case. I must have been all over the place because the security guy eventually picked me up and literally carried me downstairs to my room. A make-up artist on the team finally staggered back to her room to pack, but she ended up passing out and wasn't seen again that day – even on the tour bus. She simply didn't make it. In the end, she had to get a flight to Glasgow just to make our next gig.

Meanwhile, I was thrown on the bus and went right to my bunk. Yes, I knew I had another gig that night, but I also knew that I could sleep most of the day if I needed to. In those days, it didn't seem to matter how much I partied on tour, I was always fine the next night as long as I got enough sleep in between. I'm pretty sure that wouldn't be the case these days, but back then I had the constitution of an ox. Nowadays, I get out of breath going to and from the Co-op.

I wasn't the only one in the band who liked to let off steam by any means. We were in Moscow once, playing a private gig very close to the Kremlin, and there was plenty of drinking on that trip, after the gig. It was our very last show before the Christmas break of 2007, and after a whole year of working hard, we were ready for a couple of weeks of just chilling with friends and family.

Back at the hotel, after the show, drinks were flowing. In fact, we all got pretty steaming with the promoters of the gig in the hotel bar. As it got later and later, some of the dancers went out to clubs and Nicola, Cheryl and Kimberley gradually ebbed off from the bar to bed. Meanwhile, Nadine and I stayed on, drinking and chatting away. At one point, Nadine disappeared, God knows where to. I thought she'd gone to bed too, but a little while later she was back again, ready for 'one more' drink.

In the midst of all of this, in through the door of the hotel walks Boy George, heading for the lifts. Now, there was a bit of history between George and us; bad blood, you might say. So, being in the lively state that I was, I decided to collar him.

'Oi, you!' I shouted across the room.

George had been rude about us at the Vodafone Live Music Awards that year. We'd been performing at the awards, singing live, as we always did at our shows.

'I don't know why they're here,' he'd said. 'They're just a bunch of pretty girls prancing around on the stage.'

Afterwards, when a journalist had asked me what I'd thought about his comment, I'd said something like, 'How would he know anyway? He's too busy sweeping shit off the streets of New York!'

This was in reference to the community service George was ordered to do after pleading guilty to falsely reporting a burglary at his apartment in Manhattan, where police officers found cocaine. I also suggested he might be jealous of our make-up as it was better than his.

Once I got George's attention in the bar, I said, 'I think we ought to have a little chat, don't you?'

'Well, if it's about what I think it's about, I'm really sorry,' he said. 'I didn't mean it; it was just banter.'

George ended up joining us for drinks, and we ended up having a good chat and putting all the bitchiness behind us.

The night went on and on until our tour manager Drew appeared to inform us that we had half an hour. I wondered for a moment what he meant. Was Drew telling us we had half an hour until the bar closed? Apparently not. It turned out that he meant half an hour before we left for the airport to travel back to London. Half an hour!

Poor Drew. Besides having to pin me down, plus Nadine who'd been on several wanders around the hotel, some of the dancers hadn't arrived back from whatever bar or club they'd gone off to. On top of that, he had to get the rest of the girls out of bed. This was never easy at the best of times, especially after a night of heavy drinking. It must have been like herding cats.

Even though I hadn't even packed when Drew made his announcement, Nadine and I were oblivious to the urgency of the situation.

'Shall we have one for the road?' I suggested.

'Yeah, why not?' Nadine said.

Eventually, I made it back to my room, where I drunkenly threw my stuff into a bag. By the time I got back downstairs, Drew had located the missing dancers, but Nadine had gone AWOL again. By some miracle, we all ended up in cars on our way to the airport, and at the time I remember thinking I didn't feel that drunk. This was obviously an illusion because when we pulled up at the airport, I got it into my head that we were pulling up outside the BBC.

'Oh God, don't tell me we've got another gig to do,' I said. 'What the hell are we doing here? Drew! Drew! We've gone to the wrong place. This is the BBC.'

I wasn't the only one who was confused. Nadine and I were in separate vehicles, and, of course, the last two to get out of them. Nadine eventually got out of her car, but instead of making her way into the airport terminal, she got into the car I was in.

'OK, let's go!' she said to the driver. 'Drive on!'

And he did, with a desperate Drew running after us.

I'm not sure where she thought she was heading, but I do remember that the two of us were talking absolute bollocks.

For me, the best part of any event, show, video shoot or wild night out was always when I got home. Taking my eyelashes and make-up off and getting into the shower was always absolute heaven.

CHAPTER
THIRTEEN

Today my friend Mousey visited me at my mum's and did my hair. I think I just needed a bit of a boost and to feel a bit more human again, so she came up to do some extensions and a bit of colour. I've actually known Sarah for years, and it was through her that I met my long-term boyfriend, Tommy Crane. In fact, I've always called her Mousey because that was Tom's nickname for her.

Before I met Tom, I hadn't been the luckiest in love. Being insecure, as I was, often led me to make the wrong choices. I didn't really enjoy being on my own, so I'd tended to end up going from one boyfriend to the next, just to avoid feeling lonely. Look, I certainly wasn't the first girl in the world to dive headlong into a rebound relationship, but I sure had my fair share of them in my younger years. I think of myself as a trusting soul, so when, in the past, boys cheated on me or ended things with me, I'd feel horribly let down. The trouble was, instead of realising that the guy in question just wasn't right for me, my inner critic was always there on my shoulder, convincing me that there was something wrong with me and that it was all my fault.

I think by the time I met Tom, I'd grown quite a bit. Perhaps achieving a certain level of success in my career had given me the strength and self-belief to know what was acceptable and what wasn't. I wasn't prepared to let guys walk all over me any more, and that felt like a good place to be.

Mousey and I first met way back in the *Popstars: The Rivals* days. She was assisting hairdresser Mark Anderson on the show, and I recall doing a photoshoot with her on board even before the final girl band had been chosen, let alone named. It all got quite complicated, swapping out different girls in various shots, to make up all the different combinations of what the band might finally be. Consequently, it was somewhat stressful for Sarah and the team who were pulling all the looks together for the photos.

Sarah and I got on really well once *Popstars: The Rivals* was over. In fact, she started working with us on our video shoots and was there right from the 'Sound of the Underground' video. If ever drinks were happening after a shoot, or there was a party going on, Sarah and I would often end up hanging out together. That was when and how I started to get to know her group of friends, one of whom was a good-looking DJ called Tom.

Now, I didn't realise this at the time, but Tommy had a bit of a crush on me, so of course told Mousey about it. Being the sneaky matchmaker that she is, Mousey always tipped Tommy off about the dates and times I was coming into her salon in Regent Street to get my hair done. Then, while I was mid-hairdo, he always magically turned up, playing the innocent and pretending that his visit to the salon while I was there was purely coincidental.

'Oh, hi, girls,' he'd say. 'Just dropped in on the off-chance.'

Of course, Mousey was behind it, knowing that once I'd finished getting my hair done, we'd all end up going for drinks together.

It was undoubtedly Tommy who was doing all the chasing, but then again I probably didn't put up too much of a fight about it.

The hair salon was like a big social scene. Whenever I was in, everyone who worked there would end up going for drinks after, and out of that, a broader circle of people began to appear. In the end, it was one huge group with various offshoots and bubbles. I suppose at this time I wasn't hanging out with my bandmates so often. Of course, there were times when we were all together at one event or another, but our social lives seemed like they were worlds apart. It wasn't really anyone's fault; it was just the way things were. It felt more natural to me to hang out with my own friends.

Last night Mousey and I got together, and we tried to come up with a few stories about this era for the book. We ended up howling with laughter when we realised that quite a few of them weren't necessarily suitable for sharing. There were undoubtedly a few nights when I overdid it and ended up needing assistance to get out of a club and into the sanctuary of a waiting car. I do recall being helped down the staircase of one particular club, and on that occasion I was like Bambi on ice – not a good look, for sure! Thank God for the enormous security guard who let me lean on his shoulder as we went.

One night, we were out at a club, which was just opposite the salon, with Tommy in attendance. We'd been friendly for a while by now, and a bit flirty, but so far nothing had happened between us.

I remember that night he'd been on a serious downer about something and I'd ended up being a bit of a shoulder for him to cry on. At one point, I gave him a little peck on the mouth and told him not to worry, that everything would be all right. That kiss, I guess, was all the spark that was needed. It was clear that Tom was into me, so I encouraged him over to an area in the club where it was a little bit darker and more private. I mean, if I was going to be playing tonsil hockey with a guy in the middle of a bar, the last thing I wanted was to get papped doing it. Before long, the two of us were having a proper kiss, and something told me that this moment was going to lead me somewhere. I didn't know quite where at the time; all I knew was that it just felt right. It was pretty electric between us.

Of course, despite my attempts to be discreet that night, Mousey caught us mid-kiss, although she didn't seem all that surprised on her discovery. Funny that!

From then on, we hung out more and more, and there were various bubbles of friends we went out with. Greg Burns, the Capital Radio DJ, was someone I often hung out with around that time. He was always up for going out, and because his radio show went out in the early evening, he rarely had to be up early in the morning. He'd always come to Winter Wonderland on Hyde Park with me and was the only one who wasn't afraid to join me on the big, scary rides, which I loved. Nick Ede, who's a well-known PR, culture and charity expert, was also a friend who I hung out with a lot at that point in my life. He's a great guy and so much fun.

Around that time, I spent a lot of time at The May Fair Hotel; in fact, it became a home from home. The amount of partying we did in that place was nobody's business. In fact, Mousey says she can't even walk in the place any more, because the familiar smell of it makes her feel slightly sick. She actually feels anxiety at the thought of it. I do recall one party that seemed to go on and on, and there were all sorts of fun and games happening. We drank, we played Twister, we drank more, we had a water fight. Tommy and I ended up wrestling in the wet room and almost flooding the bathroom. I think we'd been going on and off for about two days when we were asked to move suites, I guess so they could clean the one we were in as it was due to be occupied. It's funny when I look back on those times now. It all seems quite reckless and crazy, but it was merely stuff that happened in the moment. We were young and doing well in our careers, and we didn't always think about the consequences of our actions back then.

I was always play-fighting with Tommy, and sometimes it got out of hand, especially when there had been alcohol involved. One night, Tommy and I were wrestling, again at The May Fair Hotel, when I took a tumble off the bed, slipped and twisted my ankle. My whole foot was in agony, but I didn't think it was anything too terrible.

'I'll just keep it raised up,' I told everyone. 'I think it's just a sprain.'

I was still in pain the next day, and due to walk the red carpet at a film premiere, so in the end, we called out a doctor.

I was literally in the middle of having my hair and make-up done as the doc checked me over.

'You've broken it,' he said. 'You've broken one of the metatarsal bones. We need to get you to the hospital.'

'No, I've got no time,' I said. 'I've got a film premiere!'

Not to be deterred, I somehow still made it to that bloody red carpet. The stylist changed my shoes to ones with straps so I could get my foot in them. It was, by then, black and blue. I hobbled down the carpet, clinging on to Sundraj, our publicist, looking as slinky as I possibly could while smiling through gritted teeth.

The other problem was, the doctor had put me on some powerful painkillers and, me being me, I failed to factor that in when I had a few drinks at the after-party. As well as the pain in my foot, I was in a really tight dress, and all of a sudden I felt horribly sick. In fact, at one point, I thought I was going to faint.

I did finally make it to the hospital the next day, where I had an X-ray. I left wearing one of those air boots until it was suitably healed.

Things progressed quite quickly with Tommy. Romance, I mean. It seemed as though one minute we were having that not-so-secret kiss in the club opposite Mousey's salon and the next Tommy was moving in with me. At the time, it didn't feel strange at all; it just felt right. Once Tommy had stayed over a few nights, that was it. We were practically joined at the hip, and he never really left my place. Sometimes he went back home for a couple of days, but he'd soon be back at mine because we enjoyed one another's company so much. It was that magical time when you're falling in love with someone. We just wanted to be together the whole time, and when we weren't, it felt as though something was missing.

Even when he did plan to go home for a time, there was always some reason why he ended up staying. Like the time he ate a batch of bad oysters in Selfridges' restaurant, and couldn't leave my house for a few days, for obvious reasons.

Tommy was only my third proper relationship, but there was something different about us than there had been with the others. I think what I liked most about him was his sense of humour. He made me laugh, which I loved, and he always seemed to be happy. I suppose that was one of the reasons I was content for things to move as fast as they did, and for him to be living at my place. I was just so comfortable having him around. There were differences in us, of course. While Tommy was a glass-half-full type of guy, I was very much a glass-half-empty person. In some ways, though, he was like the male version of me. He was my best friend.

I was just completing on a new place when Tommy and I got together. It had taken me absolutely ages to find the perfect home in north London. While it had lots of character and great features, there was a ton of renovation to do before it was transformed into my dream home.

As is often the case, the building work took so much longer than we thought it would. Hence, Tommy and I spent those first crucial few months together living in disarray and chaos. We started off trying to be organised, but things deteriorated fast. Instead of renting somewhere or booking into a hotel, I decided that we should live in the house while much of the work was being done. That's not easy when you're living in one bedroom, and there's no proper kitchen. All we had was a fridge and a tiny bit of countertop. When we weren't eating out at restaurants, we were eating cold snacks or grilling something on the one piece of kitchen equipment we possessed – a George Foreman grill. Either that or we were ordering take-out. After a while, I started to feel very unhealthy. The day was saved when our tour manager gave us an old microwave. Suddenly, we could actually eat hot food at home again that hadn't been delivered in a box.

For me, it was a tough thing to go through at the start of a relationship. This was supposed to be the honeymoon period. Sometimes it was everything but that, with all the stress and strains of the renovation. I don't think it was the best start to our relationship, especially with me being in a high state of stress all the time while trying to maintain a busy work schedule.

I loved living in Hampstead, but there was never much privacy there. My dog Claude and I only had to step out of the house to find ourselves being snapped by the paparazzi. I know it's part of the package when you're in a pop band as big as we were at the time, but sometimes that didn't make it any easier. I also felt like I had to be on my guard, even just popping out to get some milk at the local shop.

Those were the days of big photoshoots in *Hello!* and *OK!* magazines, and as a so-called celebrity couple, Tommy and I were asked to appear in a few 'at home' articles, with fancy photoshoots to go along with them. Tommy hated those shoots and did everything he could to get out of being in the photos. He'd always try to feature in the least amount of shots he possibly could, which made me smile.

I guess things were going on very nicely, but our crazy and sometimes erratic working lives often got in the way of a smooth existence. There were definite bumps. Tommy worked at Mahiki, which is a cocktail bar and nightclub in Mayfair, famous for its celebrity guest list. Quite often he'd end up staying for staff drinks at the end of the night, which was tough when I was due an early morning start, and he was rolling in at 5am. It must have been equally difficult for him while I was away touring and he was left to his own devices at home.

Tommy's proposal of marriage was very romantic, although it did involve him telling me to 'Shut up!'

We were on holiday in the Maldives at the time. It was New Year's Eve and the end of a decade. We'd spent the last few hours of 2010 enjoying a beautiful dinner on the beach, and then headed for cocktails. Eventually, we found our spot on the beach, both wearing silly hats, gearing up to see in the new year and watch the fireworks. I remember lying back and taking in the night sky – it looked amazing. In fact, I was so overcome with it, I couldn't stop talking about how beautiful the stars and the sky were. I was completely oblivious to the fact Tom was trying to say something. In fact, I was still banging on when the count-down to midnight began.

'Ten, nine, eight …'

'Babe, will you just shut up and let me speak,' Tom said. He pulled a huge box out of his pocket and took out a ring. 'You're my best friend, and I love you,' he said, getting down on one knee. 'Will you marry me?'

I wasn't expecting it at all. And although Tom stumbled over his words a little, they were sweet and heartfelt. He hadn't rehearsed any kind of big speech. Instead, he was simply saying how he really felt. How could I say no?

That moment was like something out a romantic movie. In fact, I find it very hard to watch soppy romantic moments in films these days, especially moments when someone tells their lover that they are also their best friend. That's a phrase that always comes back to me, thinking about that night with Tommy. I find it difficult to hear now. I've always believed that you have to be somebody's best friend to want to marry them because that's the person you're going to spend the most minutes, hours and days of your life with from then on in.

Even as time went on, it didn't seem to matter how turbulent our relationship became; we were OK while we were still best friends. I still think of what might have been.

CHAPTER
FOURTEEN

I t sometimes surprises me, the things that really get me down while living with this illness. Of course, there's the obvious stuff, like thinking about my own mortality, and the relentless treatment and the pain that often comes with it. One of the things that is particularly shitty is the loss of independence. As you've learned reading this, I was out in the world and independent from quite a young age, so to feel that slipping away from me is hard.

Actually, it's not even just slipping away; it's been bloody well been snatched away. It's a hard reality to face, but because of the tumour on my brain, it's been decided that I should not live on my own. Of course, having just moved into a new apartment and feeling a little better about how this was all going has meant this is a real blow. Mum is going to stay with me, and I know that's for the best, but it's still a hard pill to swallow. I'm not even allowed to drive now, which is really kicking a person while they're down. I guess it's not rocket science to learn that a person with a tumour on their brain isn't the best person to be behind the wheel, in charge of a fast-moving vehicle.

I suppose with getting the apartment I felt like I was moving forwards towards something. Despite having cancer, I've been living day-to-day rather than giving in to it. Now, I feel like my bubble has burst, to be honest.

I'm multitasking today. I'm making a roast dinner and trying to sort out my dressing room at the apartment, while at the same time trying to get some work done on my book. As you can imagine, writing a whole book is a hard thing to do in my current situation. I have a friend helping me; a writer called Terry Ronald. Before Terry was a writer, he worked with Girls Aloud as a vocal arranger and coach on many of our tours and TV appearances over the years. So he's known me for a very long time, which helps.

Meanwhile, my mum is pottering around somewhere, doing her own thing. Right now, I'm writing this reclining on my zebra-print chaise longue. I've had it for years – since I was living in Camden – so it's seen me through a lot. The poor thing has been moved from one house to another on numerous occasions, has had cats lying on it and dogs jumping all over it, and has been thoroughly cleaned multiple times. Somehow, it's survived all that. It's still here in all its velvety, quirky beauty and I still love it.

For me, being in a band and becoming successful was never really about fame or being a pop star; what really drove me was the idea of gaining recognition for something I was good at and that I loved. It was the sense of achievement rather than the fame I craved. Even now, I'd still love for people to see what I'm like behind closed doors and how passionate I am about making music. How I sit in my bedroom making the best of my limited knowledge of technology, creating songs, playing my guitars, and writing melodies, for no other reason than the joy of creating something. For me, all the fame and the glitter was secondary. Don't get me wrong, I knew how lucky I was, but I really think I could have done without all that as long as I was able to sing and make music and be recognised for it.

As far as recognition goes, one of the highlights of being in Girls Aloud was in 2009, when we won a BRIT award. We'd been nominated for Best British Group in 2008, but lost out to Arctic Monkeys, and also in 2009, when Elbow took the prize. At the 2009 awards show, however, we did the most spectacular live performance of 'The Promise'. We then clinched the award for Best British Single.

That had been another single where there were late changes. They were obviously worth it in the end, but everything was very last minute. With one week to go until we were due to film the video, we still didn't have an idea for what it might be. Nobody did. The label had asked Trudy Bellinger to make the video – she'd made 'The Show', 'Walk This Way' and 'Sexy! No No No …' for us, but we couldn't think of anything exciting for the concept. It got so tight that our stylist walked from the project, saying it was impossible to turn the wardrobe around in time for the shoot. Eventually, Peter's partner David Lawson came up with the idea of the drive-in and the glamorous 1960s' girl-group throwback, and from that moment we were all systems go. There was no time for proper costumes, though. Those fabulous gold dresses were actually just bits of material pinned at the back, and most of the choreography was done on the day. The night before we shot the video, we were called back to Xenomania to record a key change for a dramatic last chorus. This became one of my favourite moments live, as I always added my own soaring ad lib into the final chorus. I only wish I'd put it on the actual recording. The song ended up going to number one, and was our second biggest selling single after 'Sound of the Underground'.

Winning the BRIT for 'The Promise' was one of the biggest moments of my life … I'm sure all the other girls will say the same. As usual, I was the first to grab the award when we got up there on stage, holding it aloft and screaming, 'It's about time!' This was quickly followed by, 'I think I've just wet myself!' It was such a mad moment.

Not long after that, we embarked on our fifth tour, Out of Control, and we opened up for Coldplay at Wembley Stadium at Chris Martin's request, which were the last two things we did before Girls Aloud embarked on what would turn into a three-year hiatus. Apart from anything else, I think we were all exhausted. We'd been working for seven years non-stop by then: single, video, promo, album, tour, over and over. Girls Aloud were a machine, and there didn't seem to be any sign of us slowing down. It was time to take a break.

When we eventually reunited, three years later, we released a career-spanning greatest-hits album, *Ten* to celebrate ten years of the band, and embarked on one final tour. Singing in front of all the fans again was extremely emotional for all of us, especially during the final show, where we ended up blubbing at the old footage of the band, flashing up on the screens above us. We'd all agreed that it was time to say goodbye at the end of the tour. I know Nadine wasn't as happy with the decision, and I probably could have gone either way, but when it came down to it, it just wasn't the same any more. Our collective hearts weren't in it.

As amazing as it had all been, it wasn't always quite as fabulous as it looked. We were often being rushed here, pushed there, bouncing from interview to TV show and then back to another interview. It's not like we were hard done by or being mistreated, far from it; it's just the way things were when there was something big to promote. A lot of the time, we were working until we could hardly keep our eyes open. In those seven years, everyone wanted a piece of Girls Aloud, and as long as that was the case, the band would carry on being successful. We all knew we were leading a charmed life compared to most, and I always tried to appreciate that, but I didn't feel glamorous a lot of the time, I can tell you. Yes, there were moments of glamour, lots of them, but day-to-day it was often hard to keep up. Once you had your hair and make-up on, you'd step out on stage looking a million dollars, but sometimes underneath you'd be thinking, Jesus, I'm knackered! How am I going to get through this? It was usually the rush of adrenaline that got me through, especially during a live show.

The thing that used to upset me most about the constant rushing around is when I had to disappoint fans. Wherever we went, there were young people wanting autographs and photos. Every time we stepped out of a building, there they were. It was always lovely when we could stop for a chat and to sign something for them, but bloody hideous when we were running late and dragged away by tour managers and had to jump into a car without a word, or maybe just a quick wave. The problem was, our schedule during promotion was always tightly packed. We'd often be rushing out of one interview or TV appearance on our way to something else with no time to spare, perhaps even to catch a train or a flight. Our tour managers had the unenviable job of making sure all five of us were exactly where we needed to be at the right time, which often meant rushing us out of buildings and into cars whether or not we wanted to stop and chat. Still, I hated seeing the sadness and disappointment on the faces of these young fans when I couldn't stop. I always wanted someone to physically drag me away, so they would know it wasn't my fault that I couldn't stop and talk to them. It made me feel dreadful, and I'd end up apologising for England. It's funny – for so much of my life I've felt like I always had to explain myself and to apologise to people over and over. I don't know why. I should have been able to tell the fans that I loved them and walk off to my next job, like a professional. They'd have understood. I never could, though. Whatever that thing was that the other girls seemed to have, I didn't have it.

My fans – the Sarah fans – have always been brilliant, and have done so much for me. The Sarah Harding Addicts in particular, as well as all of my other fabulous long-time supporters: Kelly, Chris, Sammie, Shanna, Holly, Hannah, Hollie, and the two Sarahs! They have always been there for me in difficult times. They also understand when I go quiet or disappear off the radar for a while. They know now that I can't be on social media because I'm not well and I can't really deal with all that stuff. In fact, they're so important to me that I asked the Sarah Harding Addicts, Natasha and Claire, if they would kindly make a contribution to my book.

This is what they wrote for me …

For us, Sarah always felt like the most down-to-earth member of Girls Aloud. She was a straight-talking northerner, she loved animals and was charismatic. OK, we're not going to lie, she was also hot, which was undoubtedly a major contributing factor given that we were a pair of gay girls. The funny thing is, neither of us was the type to be massive fans of anyone before that. Yes, we both loved pop music, but we didn't have any particular icons or idols to speak of. Sarah was different. It all started when we went to our first Girls Aloud concert. For us, Sarah stood out on stage with such presence – and what a voice! As well as that, there was something fascinating about her background and where she came from; the fact that she'd stuck to her guns and fought to achieve her dream for so long before she got a break. That idea that a young woman could have such ambitions, and execute them through sheer force of will, was, to us, inspiring.

Her on-stage persona seemed wild and crazy – she wasn't your average pop girl band type, for sure – but our first meeting with Sarah changed our view completely. She came across as kind and sweet and had lots of time for her fans. After that, it was Sarah Harding the person we became fans of, rather than Sarah the pop star.

We started the website 'Sarah Harding Addicts' in 2006, just through chatting on the Girls Aloud official forum. Someone mentioned that Sarah didn't have a website, and that was it, we were off. When Twitter got big in 2009, we started a Twitter account for the site and then an Instagram page. Sarah was aware of what we were doing from very early on, and she's always been hugely supportive.

As well as Sarah, we also loved the band's music. Girls Aloud are always on in our house and in the car. The only criticism we had was that Sarah never seemed to get enough solo lines. OK, so we might be biased, but to us, she had the best voice, and we always wanted to hear more from her.

Hearing the news of Sarah's breast cancer broke out hearts. Having been through it with family members, and with personal experience, it really hit home. Having that knowledge of all the stuff that goes hand-in-hand with breast cancer gave us an insight into what Sarah was going through: the ups and downs of it, the fear of the unknown, the apprehension around each new blood test and scan. When we heard the word 'advanced' concerning her illness, we were scared and gutted for her. That's the one word you just don't want to hear when you're going through cancer treatment.

We recently made Sarah a book of messages and support from all her many fans and well-wishers, full of photographs and about 350 *messages. We know she received it on a day when she met up with all the other girls recently and was over the moon with it. That meant everything to us. She even sent us a lovely thank you card.*

Sarah has meant so much to her fans over the years. She's always had time for us, and never takes us for granted. All we can do now is show our support and make sure she knows how much we love her.

—*Claire Hill and Natasha Young – Sarah Harding Addicts*

CHAPTER
FIFTEEN

Aside from singing, I think acting was always on the cards for me. When I drew that picture of myself in front of a camera as a child, to me it meant acting.

Just before our hiatus, I'd been offered the chance to try it, and grabbed it with both hands. I still loved singing and had no intention of giving it up, but I'd also loved drama and acting from when I was very young.

My first proper role was playing Jade Jennings in a British thriller called *Bad Day*. I suppose it could be described as a female version of *Layer Cake*, only with a much lower budget. For that role, I wore a long brunette wig, which would serve to cover up my distinctive blonde crop.

Bad Day set my foot on the ladder, and in 2009 I got a part in the BBC film *Freefall*, written by Dominic Savage. The film was set around the start of the financial crisis of 2008. It starred Dominic Cooper as this bad-boy mortgage broker, who sells mortgages to people he knows can't afford to pay them. Throughout the film, he gets more and more out of control until everything collapses around him. I played his character's girlfriend, Sam, who was a beautician, and it was a pretty good shout for me. The role wasn't huge, but people were saying I was good in it. In fact, *Company* magazine said that I had real acting potential and that I was convincing. I was well happy with that!

I'd been juggling quite a lot of filming with my Girls Aloud duties. I worried that it was putting some of the girls' noses out of joint that I was doing other stuff. I remember feeling bad about it, but I didn't want to miss out on what I saw as great opportunities.

Once we'd taken our break, I got a part in *St Trinian's 2: The Legend of Fritton's Gold*. As a band, we'd had a cameo in the first *St Trinian's* film, but this was, for me, a proper role, and my favourite of all the acting parts I did. In it, I played teenage tearaway Roxy, a new student at the school. I guess you could say it was typecasting, with me being cast as a rebellious type, although Roxy was a lot moodier and cooler than me. Marc Robinson from Globe at Universal brilliantly persuaded Ricky Wilson from the Kaiser Chiefs to play the part of my boyfriend in the movie. He and his band had been guests on our Christmas TV special, *The Girls Aloud Party*, along with James Morrison.

During the *St Trinian's* filming, I was always being told I had to play it down and not get too excitable.

'Can you be less animated?' the director would say during takes.

Christ, can you imagine? Me, the world's worst fidgeting firecracker, trying to calm it down and be less animated; it wasn't easy, I can tell you.

The directors explained to me that big head movements and hand gestures would read ten times more prominent on a full-size cinema screen. It was a huge learning curve, but I took it all in and found my way. One of the best things about it was working with our producers, Xenomania, to record some solo tracks for the *St Trinian's* soundtrack – one of them being a cover of David Bowie's classic, 'Boys Keep Swinging'.

The film didn't get the most outstanding reviews, but we had a fun time doing it, and a great cast including Colin Firth, David Tennant, and Rupert Everett as Miss Camilla Fritton.

Acting was something I could look to once Girls Aloud had come to an end, and it's something I'd still love to do now if I could. The only downside of it for me was my 'red light fever'. I'm fine when I'm rehearsing or when I don't know the camera is on, but I do suffer from nerves as soon as I see the camera is rolling. It was the same when I was in the recording studio; I tense up as soon as we do a take and I never sing as well as I did when we were just doing a practice run. Down the line, when I appeared in a few episodes of *Coronation Street*, the red light fever was most definitely there. It's such an iconic show, an institution, and when you're going on as a short-term character, it's hard to get into your stride. That was a tough gig for me because it was like I was playing a part that wasn't a million miles away from the real me. You might imagine that it would be an easy thing to do, but I think I'd have found it more comfortable playing someone who was the complete opposite of myself. Even if I'd had different-coloured hair or a foreign accent, I'd have settled into it more.

I played Joni, Robert Preston's wife. She came in all guns blazing, looking for her old man on the cobbles and finding him in a relationship with Tracy Barlow. Corrie is shot at a very fast pace, and they literally threw me in at the deep end. In fact, my very first day on set was pretty much all screaming, crying and slapping. Still, I enjoyed working with Kate Ford, who played Tracy; she's a lovely girl, and we ended up having a proper giggle together. It's funny, back when I filmed *Bad Day*, I had pages of dialogue to learn for a scene on the phone in the back of a car, and I was fine with it. Still, on Corrie, after two or three lines with the iconic Rita Sullivan in The Kabin, my knees turned to jelly.

CHAPTER
SIXTEEN

When Tommy went to Ibiza for the season to DJ, I was left to my own devices in London. He'd been away working in the past, but after four years together we'd started to grow apart. I'd always trusted him when he was off doing gigs, especially as it was usually one or two nights and he'd be back again. Now he was away for longer and longer periods, and with things the way they were, my mind was working overtime, wondering what the hell he might be up to. It wasn't as if I could get over there to see him, because I was busy filming *Run for Your Wife* with Danny Dyer, Denise Van Outen and Neil Morrissey. During the filming, I'd been hanging out with Danny and Neil, and there'd been a fair bit of drinking going on. In fact, my drinking got a bit heavier during that period, especially given the situation between Tommy and me. I missed him, and I found it very tough, but instead of absence making the heart grow fonder, the distance seemed to be driving a wedge between us.

At one point during my filming schedule, Tommy came to visit me in the hotel where I was staying. He wanted a romantic night in, but I was so tired after a long day, I just wanted to get into the bath and go to bed. In the meantime, I got a message from someone inviting me for drinks in the bar with the director and some of the producers. They wanted to have a chat about how the day had gone, and what the plans were for the following day's shoot. I wasn't feeling it at all, but I knew I had to keep everyone happy and play the game.

'We'll have to go down there,' I told Tommy. 'It's kind of expected.'

Tom was having none of it, refusing to go. Inevitably, we ended up having an almighty row. I suppose it had been coming for a long time, but it wasn't pretty. In the end, I asked him to leave the hotel.

'I haven't got anywhere to go,' he said.

My house was in Buckinghamshire by that point, and as we were in west London, home was hardly around the corner.

'Tom, you've got your family and all the friends you lived with in London. You need to go and stay with one of them.'

I know I should have calmed down and made it up with him, but it came after so many weeks of frustration and feeling abandoned, I wasn't thinking straight. I guess that was the moment when I finally pushed Tommy away. It's something I've never really forgiven myself or taken responsibility for. I've never stopped blaming myself. Losing him was one of the biggest mistakes of my life, but we just couldn't seem to find a way through the impasse. I sometimes think that if it hadn't been for that night, we might still be in one another's life. Instead, that's when it all fell apart.

Talking about this brings up all sorts of sad thoughts in me. The idea that I'll never have children. That one came to me the other day when I was talking to Cheryl on the phone. I was saying how we never thought Nadine would be the first one of us to have a child, and that now three of them have kids. It might seem odd to worry about not having children when I don't even know how much of a life I have left, but it's there. The truth is, even if my prognosis was better, it still wouldn't be on the cards because of all the chemotherapy I've had. That treatment, harsh as it is, will have killed any chance I might have had. It's making me cry just thinking about it. I wanted all that back when I was with Tom. I'd planned it out because I'd never before felt anything like I did for him. If I have regrets, these are my biggest ones. And no, it wasn't all perfect between us. It was often a case of hero to zero as far as our relationship went, from both sides. But everything came from love. There was always love. I knew, even when Tommy was angry with me, he still loved me. He wanted me to be better and kinder to myself. I think that me being me, in the industry I was in, pulled us apart in the end. I was just too much for him to handle, and so I lost the love of my life. And my best friend.

When you're in the public eye, you sometimes have to make personal sacrifices. It's one of the payoffs for all the great stuff it can bring. You have to accept that, good or bad, you're not going to have the same life that the people outside the bubble of fame have. It's that simple.

I hate that about fame and celebrity. Is it naive or selfish to want to be able to do the thing you love and still want a normal life? Maybe. I have craved normality. I do want a normal life. A life that now seems even more precious.

It's just my mum and me now, and I guess that's the way it's going to be from here on in. OK, so I've got enough going on without having a man around to deal with, but still … I sometimes think if I'd have done things differently; if I'd not given in to, or played up to, that caricature of 'Sarah from Girls Aloud' so often. It could be different now, couldn't it? There were too many occasions when I took out my own insecurities on people I loved and still do love. If I hadn't messed up so many times, I might be happy now. I really think I could have been. Who knows?

The next time I saw Tommy after our break-up was at the wedding of our mutual friend, Michelle Gayle. Tommy was quite frosty, and when we did try to talk, he got tearful.

Since then, we've tried being friends. It's always ended up turning into something more but stopping short of getting back together. It hurt then, and it still hurts now. When Tommy and I broke up, I didn't just lose him, I lost a family. There was a divide with our group of friends, with most of them going out to Ibiza to watch him play. This was something we'd always done as a group, but I wasn't part of it any more. Whenever I go to the island now, I go with my new group of friends, and I avoid the clubs where Tom is playing. On the odd occasion that I have, he seems to be conscious of the fact I'm there and has let it be known to some of my friends that he can't concentrate. So I stay away.

After Tommy and I broke up, I went into a tailspin. I was out of control, and however much I tried to pull myself together and put forward a confident exterior, inside I was a mess. It was the start of a dark, difficult period for me. One I almost didn't come back from.

The split from Tommy left me broken, and I suppose that was the time I abused myself the most. I found myself in Ibiza, having just finished filming *Run for Your Wife*.

I'd gone to the island with two of my girlfriends, and we were staying at Pikes Hotel, which is where the video for Wham's 'Club Tropicana' was filmed – in the countryside near San Antonio. Pikes has got quite a name for itself, being one of the most infamous hotels on the island, with a reputation for hedonism and some pretty wild behaviour during the 1980s. It's generally thought of as a bit of a hot spot for the rich and famous. I had a bungalow there, and the three of us were having fun, listening to music, playing games and generally relaxing. We were all drinking a lot, but I was getting stupidly drunk – spiralling out of control, you might say. Meanwhile, my friends, knowing what I was going through, were doing their utmost to keep an eye on me and make sure I didn't go over the edge, but, to be honest, they were fighting a losing battle.

At the time, Jaime and Lois Winstone were over on the island. One night they invited my girlfriends and me to join them for a bit of a party, but my friends didn't want me to leave the hotel. I ended up at the hotel's Freddie Mercury tribute night with some other mates, wearing a moustache. Later I found myself dancing my ass off behind the decks with 2manyDJs, who are a left-of-centre dance duo of brothers from Belgium. I was dripping with sweat with make-up running down my face, having a great time. It should have ended there, really. Instead, a few of us went upstairs to someone's flat for a while, then it was back down to the party. That's when it started to get a bit messy. It was really late by this time, and time to go to bed, but I didn't!

By then, my girlfriends were worried about me. I'd texted to say I was on my way back but then got chatting to a couple who'd been partying hard. By that time, I was getting a bit emotional. I guess that's what sometimes happens when you're upset or distraught about something. You drink to forget, and it's great when you're on the way up, but when you're coming back down the other side at the end of the party, everything just seems a hundred times worse. I remember a few songs being played that night that made me nostalgic and sent me on a downer. 'It Must Be Love' by Madness was one; Tom and I had talked about that song being the first dance at our wedding. The couple I was hanging out with had a little bit of everything on them and were happy to share.

'I'm usually quite picky, but at the moment I'll try whatever you've got,' I told them.

You can just imagine what kind of mess I was in when I did finally get back to my friends. The next day wasn't at all pretty.

This continued when I was back in the UK, with me going completely over the top. There was usually someone on hand offering something to help ease the pain. It got so bad that I had to have a couple of girlfriends stay at the house with me, just to make sure I was OK. I wasn't sleeping properly or eating. I was on a treadmill of booze, sleeping pills and drugs if they were around. Anything to numb the pain. Don't get me wrong, I didn't go down the dark route of heroin or anything like that, and drugs like ketamine and crystal meth scared the life out of me. I'd seen people taking ketamine in Ibiza, and watched them turn into these strange beings, once the high had subsided; sitting there, rocking like maniacs.

Still, it was bad enough, and a measure of how low I felt. If something really bad had happened to me, it most definitely would have been then. I realised then that it was literally a case of do or die, and I knew I had to take action.

CHAPTER
SEVENTEEN

My heart goes out to people, many of them in the entertainment industry, who have struggled with ongoing issues around alcohol and drugs. Some of them, like me, simply fall down during difficult times, and then do their best to deal with those times as they arise. Looking back, I probably should have given myself a bit more credit for having the balls to go and fight my demons when I did. I believe everyone who puts themselves through rehab deserves credit; it's never easy. It's even harder to talk about it honestly, but that's what I'm trying to do.

I'd never describe myself as an addict. However bad things got, I always knew when enough was enough. Still, I'm not going to lie, I've had a few stints in rehab – more than many people know about. It's something I chose to do when I felt I needed to, and even though some were more successful than others, doing it always gave me a chance to stop and take stock.

One of the rehab places I went to was based in South Africa. I chose it because it was highly commended by my psychiatrist at the time, and sold to me as a very private facility. Management even told me they had equine therapy, which unfortunately turned out not to be the case. Not a horse in sight!

When it was time to go to the airport, I was a mess. In fact, it took my driver Ray almost two hours to get me out of the house; he was virtually dragging me in the end. I was in such a state: crying, scared. I simply did not want to go. En route to the airport, I sat in the back of the car on the phone to Nicola, crying my eyes out.

'How am I going to do this, Nicola? I'm on my own … I'm doing this on my own.'

Nicola listened patiently to me; she was so supportive. I think she, like everyone, knew I needed to do something. I knew it too. It was a help just being able to talk to her on that journey to the airport because it took my mind off where I was going and what might be waiting for me. By the time I got to the airport, it was almost too late to board. I was whisked through the airport by a kind member of the Virgin airline staff, and, somehow, just about made it.

Most rehab facilities offer primary and secondary treatment. Primary treatment starts with a thorough assessment and detox. Once your body is clear of the substance, you might have one-on-one or group counselling, which shows you how addiction affects your mind and body. It can also throw up various psychological issues and triggers that go alongside addiction. It usually lasts at least thirty days, but can sometimes be much longer. With secondary treatment, you look more closely at the emotional issues and behaviour that can lead to addiction. It's less structured than primary but helps people learn how to get through their daily life without substances. This is often the time when people relapse or give up, but the idea is to learn to gradually regain more control of your life.

Much of the work in rehab facilities is done in groups, and I found it extremely difficult, sharing stories about myself in front of strangers. Still, at least in South Africa, thousands of miles away from home, I felt like nobody knew me or had preconceived ideas about who I was and what I was about. That was something which made it a little bit easier. In South Africa, I'd opted for secondary care because I wasn't a high-risk case. However, I still had to go through the primary unit to receive a medical detox. While I was there, I stayed shut in my room all day. The unit was full of serious addicts, mostly guys, and I found it very frightening. Whenever I did have to venture out, I'd have guys shouting after me, 'Hey, Blondie! Come talk to me.' That didn't help my anxiety, and in the end, I had to have a member of staff with me the whole time, like a chaperone. After three days, the team let me out, moving me into secondary care, where I joined about seven other people.

From the off, things didn't go well for me. Far from being therapeutic, I felt like we were just opening can after can of worms, raking up issues that, I felt, had nothing to do with why I was there.

One night, while we were watching a movie on the sofa, I was sharing a blanket with one of the other guys in the group. There were other people present, and it was completely innocent. When I heard one of the kitchen staff had been laughing and gossiping about a supposed romance going on, I went mad, confronting him head-on. 'How dare you say stuff like that about me? How fucking dare you? Nothing is happening, and you could get into trouble.' The damage was done, though. Any sort of involvement between residents was strictly out of bounds, and I was told I had to keep separate from the guy in question. It's called being put on boundaries, which means you can't even be in the same room at the same time, aside from in group therapy.

After that, I lost heart with the place. For better or worse, I was uninterested in what was on offer. Flower therapy, for instance, where someone would hold up a flower and ask questions like, 'How do you feel when you look at this flower? What do you see?' 'Well, it's purple, mate, purple and yellow. Beautiful colours, but it doesn't make me feel like a butterfly or anything.'

I found myself feeling desperate; kicking off about everything. The tighter the fence around me became, the harder I rebelled. In the end, word came back that my psychiatrist had given the OK to send me back to primary care.

'We don't believe you're ready for secondary care,' I was told. 'We want to send you back to the primary unit.'

I was upset with my psychiatrist for not having my back, or not at least discussing a plan with me. My options were going back to the scary primary unit for a month and then returning to the facility or leaving altogether.

'We can't help you any more,' I was told.

Now I was angry. I felt as though everyone had conspired behind my back, all happy to send me back to that terrible place without even having discussed it with me. I couldn't bear the thought of going back there. Some of the people were bloody scary, and I didn't feel I had anywhere near the same depth of problems. With no choice, I checked out of the facility and into a hotel. Not just any hotel, either, but the Four Seasons, because it was the only one I knew. The first thing I did when I got there was head to the bar and get a glass of Prosecco. I suppose it was an act of defiance on my part. I was just happy to be out of there. I wasn't going to give up on myself that easily, however. I'd done some digging around and found out that there was another rehab place in South Africa that sounded like it might suit me better. I knew it was probably going to be tough, but I was willing to give it a go.

I phoned Angela at my management and told her I'd left the original place and was going to try to get into another. Unfortunately, the new place didn't have any room for me – at least not for a couple of weeks. I considered throwing in the towel and going home, but then something clicked. If I went home now, I'd have failed. Not only that, but due to a so-called friend who'd alerted the UK press to the fact that I was in rehab, *everybody* would know I'd failed. I couldn't let that happen. In the end, I decided to stay put where I was until a place opened up – in a luxurious suite at the Four Seasons. No point in being uncomfortable, right?

While I was waiting, I became a proper little tourist, seeing all the sights: I saw Table Mountain; I wandered along the seafront and watched the seals; I did some shopping; and tried out the local food. I was on my own, and I loved it.

The second facility was better, but there were a lot more people there, so it sometimes felt a bit manic. Still, I got on with the other residents, and, although it was hard, I knew I had to try my best to get through it. The facility had a strict regimen, and it was all based around a 12-step programme. According to the programme, the way to manage an addiction is to follow the 12 steps, as well as receiving guidance from other alcoholics or addicts who have achieved what you want to achieve. Among other things, these steps include accepting that we are powerless over whatever we're addicted to. Also accepting that our lives have become unmanageable and that we should make amends to others we may have hurt. We'd get up at 6am for Reinhold Niebuhr's serenity prayer: *'God, grant me the serenity to accept the things I cannot change, the courage to change the things I can, and wisdom to know the difference.'*

Later there would be various tasks to complete throughout the day, as well as classes to attend. The classes would cover things like self-healing or therapeutic stuff. We were even asked to write our life story, which felt like an impossible task for me back then. Where the hell did I begin with that?

The African drumming classes were a riot, as were the dance classes, which sometimes took place on the pebbled beach, and always got me sweating. First thing in the morning, I'd go for a run with some of the other residents. We had 45 minutes of our own time before the day began, so a run along the beach as the sun came up was a fantastic way to start the day. I'd run past surfers and people playing in the sea with their dogs, and, seeing the beauty in things, I began to feel alive again. It was the first sense of peace and escape I'd felt in a very long time, and I had time to think about the reasons I'd taken myself there. I realised how badly I'd handled my break-up with Tommy. On Saturday night, we took it in turns to choose the evening activity. When it finally came to my turn, I knew exactly what I was going to suggest. 'Right, we're doing "Rehab's Got Talent",' I announced. 'I'm going to be the judge – let's do it!'

Some people sang, some did a bit of African dancing or drumming, and others formed a group. At the end of it, I came on as a guest performer along with a girl called Amelia, with whom I'd become friendly. Amelia played the guitar, and, unlike me, had brought hers with her. I'm not sure why, but she was only allowed to play it for an hour a week, but on that evening, she'd agreed to accompany me as a guest singer. There was no clear winner in the end; in fact, most of the acts were pretty terrible. It didn't matter though: it was just supposed to be a laugh, and that's precisely what it turned out to be.

Things started to go wrong for me when I covered for a Lithuanian stripper called Lina, who'd been hiding a phone in her bra the whole time she was there. As you can probably imagine, the use of any kind of technology or gadgets are forbidden while you're in primary rehab, so she was on shaky ground to start with. The fact that she wasn't the brightest person and kept asking people who worked at the facility for the Wi-Fi code just made things worse.

When some of us went out on a day trip, Lina decided to take a selfie of herself and me against the dramatic backdrop of some cliffs. Big mistake! Our chaperone that day was one of the mentors who I'd dubbed Captain Superman because he was always so righteous and strict. Unfortunately, he spotted something out of the corner of his eagle-eye – or at least thought he did.

'Did I see a phone just then?' he asked.

'No, what phone?' I said, not wanting the girl to get into trouble. I guess he couldn't be sure, so it didn't go any further at that time.

However, back at the facility, Lina needed to hide the phone somewhere less obvious than the inside of her bra. I offered to hide it in the area where my tuck box was kept. I'm not sure why I was willing to do it; probably because I have a naturally rebellious nature. All was quiet until the next 'housekeeping' meeting, where any in-house business, conflicts and pertinent issues are dealt with.

At that meeting, I was sitting next to Captain Superman, who had plenty to say about the suspected black-market item.

'Right, the phone,' he said. 'Raise your hands if you know about this phone.'

Almost everyone put their hands up.

'OK, does anybody know where it is?'

Nothing. It felt a bit like being at school, with Captain Superman encouraging us to own up.

'Come on, do the right thing,' he said. 'You know it's the right thing.'

In the end, I had to give it up. Captain Superman made me get up in front of everyone to go and get it. I was commended and thanked for doing the right thing, but I still got punished. I guess you could say it was all downhill from there.

After phone-gate there was sugar-gate. This was something that happened when an ice cream van pulled up outside the facility. None of us had any money, but Lina used her charm to get free ice cream from the man in the truck. In the end, a whole bunch of us were queuing up for complimentary Mr Whippy, unaware of what the consequences were going to be. The thing was, within the facility, there were people with severe eating disorders. When it got back to the mentors that some of us were scoffing shit-loads of sugar, it was deemed unfair on certain people, and we got into grief. Once again, the incident was brought up at housekeeping, with me, Lina and Amelia named as the instigators.

The three of us were put in boundaries, which meant we couldn't mix with one another, talk, go into the smoking room at the same time, or even sit near one another.

Then there was coffee-gate! During our time at the facility, we all had deadlines to do our written exercises, and deliver them on time. We were up at 6am every morning, with various chores and activities during the day, and evening meetings, which were a mini-bus ride away. It was all fine and expected in rehab, although at the time I did liken it to being in *Annie*, singing, 'It's the Hard Knock Life' to myself. All this meant that some of us were often up late into the night, getting our written stuff finished. I needed my coffee, but still always felt tired. One afternoon, I found Amelia handling what appeared to be a secret stash.

'Why are you hiding coffee?' I asked her.

'Don't tell anyone, but there's no caffeine in the evening coffee,' she said. 'It's bloody decaf.'

'WHY WOULD THEY DO THAT?' I yelled. 'I can't stay awake on my own, and I've got so much to do.'

I was already chain-smoking with all the nervous energy I had in there, so maybe shed-loads of coffee wasn't ideal. Still, all

I could think about was how exhausted I was, trying to bang out my bloody life story at midnight and beyond. The upshot was that Amelia was hiding coffee all over the place and sharing it out with those in the know, like some rich-roast drug dealer. Once again, yours truly was the one bringing it up at the next house meeting.

By then, I was quite discouraged, and, stupidly, I started to get romantically attached to somebody at the facility. I guess it was something similar to the Florence Nightingale syndrome. That's where a patient falls in love with their doctor or nurse due to the bond created between them, even though they're complete strangers.

In my case, it was another resident at the facility; a guy I thought I could help, or perhaps we thought we could help one another. Neither of the above turned out to be true. Due to our circumstances, a closeness developed between us. It's a psychological thing, really, rather than anything real. We were going through a shared experience in close quarters, day after day. I'm sure it's not the first time something like that has happened in a rehab facility, but I wish I could have seen it for what it was. We ended up leaving the facility together, and before I knew it I was back in the Four Seasons. After that, he flew back to London with me. Theo was Dutch, and was actually in recovery for addiction – much more serious than I'd previously been exposed to. In fact, once I saw him break down, I got a glimpse of something I never want to be around again. He changed completely from the guy I thought I knew, and it freaked me out.

The fight that left me black and blue with a suspected arm fracture was well-documented in the press. We'd been on a skiing holiday in Austria over Christmas and New Year, but we weren't getting on. We'd both fallen off the wagon and had a few drinks because it was Christmas. I knew in my heart that we weren't right for one another, so decided it was best to cut the trip short, for my own sake as well as his. I left to catch a flight home, leaving Theo to his own devices. While I was at the airport, I had a gin and tonic – just one – but then my flight home was cancelled. I had to go back to the hotel and face him.

When I arrived back, Theo refused to help me with my cases, and I think he'd been drinking. He became abusive and cruel, calling me a B-class singer and telling me I had no friends. He was basically throwing all my insecurities at me, so in return, I threw a cup, which missed. What can I say, I'm a thrower. It's what I do when I get angry, I throw things. I'll admit I lost it, and I'm not proud of that, but he was brutally goading me, and God was I fragile!

The scene that followed was monumental. While I struggled, Theo had me by the neck, on the floor, so I kicked him to get him off me. After that, it escalated into a full-scale fight. It was horrible. My head smashed on the floor, my arm shut in the bathroom door, and blood smeared my face. I screamed for help, but with the sound of celebratory New Year's Eve fireworks going off everywhere, nobody heard me. It culminated in me being forced outside and down the stairs.

Despite his addictions, Theo had been such a nice guy when we met. I mistakenly thought our shared experience could be a bond and that we could help one another, but it turned out to be the opposite. Still, I never imagined he could be capable of something like that.

In the end, a Swedish couple found me, hysterically crying, lying in the courtyard: dazed, bloody and bruised. They took me into their room, and I asked them to call the police.

When the police took me to the hospital, I kept asking them why they hadn't arrested Theo after what he'd done. They said I had more chance of pressing charges if I went to the hospital, and he'd also told them that it was me who'd attacked him. This is what he told the press too, that he has never been involved in a fight and was just trying to restrain me because I was attacking him. He said that I was the violent one, that I'd thrown an ashtray that had blackened his eye. He also spoke about me having done a lot of kick-boxing in the past. I certainly didn't get the chance to do any kick-boxing that night. I was too busy trying to defend myself.

I couldn't believe the mess I'd got myself into with Theo, but all I wanted now was to be safe and back at home. At the end of this whole period, I realised that I was still desperately sad about my break-up with Tommy. I'd done all this stuff to get over him: drinking, partying, then trying to get clean and going to rehab, before getting involved with someone completely unsuitable. It was a mess. The whole thing was a mess, and the lowest point of my life.

The truth was, I was all over the place – broken because I missed Tommy so much.

CHAPTER
EIGHTEEN

These days, I am more in control of what was once my addiction. I am having a glass of wine or two during all this, because it helps me relax. I'm sure some people might think that's not a great idea, but I want to try to enjoy my life. I'm at a stage now where I don't know how many months I have left. If something kills me now, it's certainly not going to be a glass of wine.

I want this Christmas to mean something and to feel special. Even the tree has to be amazing. The trouble is, everyone seems to have gone Christmas crazy this year – and extra early – so there's not much left. I suppose that's because of Covid and the lockdown. This year has been so unbelievably awful for everyone, I guess we're all just desperate to celebrate something, or at least have something to look forward to. I don't ever remember a time when Christmas felt more important. It's getting to the point where I'm starting to worry that if I don't get something sorted fast, tree-wise, I'll end up with a twig, a fairy, and a couple of baubles. If I can, I want something eight to ten feet tall – something incredibly fabulous.

Christmas is extra special to me this year because last week my doctor told me that it will probably be my last. Who knows, maybe I'll surprise everyone, but for now, that's how I'm looking at things. I don't want an exact prognosis. I don't know why anyone would want that. Comfort and being as pain-free as possible is what's important to me now. Silly little things make me happy: my lie-ins, watching *Family Guy* on TV through the night when I can't sleep, roasting a chicken for Mum and me on a Sunday, if I'm feeling up to it.

Still, I'm trying to be realistic, however hard that may be. It's for that reason that I'm trying to live and enjoy every second of my life, however long it might be. So, yes, a great big Christmas tree.

I have always loved songwriting and creating music. During the recording session for our second album, *What Will the Neighbours Say?*, we'd all got to co-write separate songs with the producers. It was an excellent way for us to get more into songwriting, and I jumped at the chance. The idea was that the tracks would be great to have for bonus tracks and B-sides for our subsequent single releases. My composition, 'Hear Me Out', was one of the tracks that ended up going on to the album, which made me very proud. I'd written the lyric about the break-out relationship with Mikey and it included my favourite lines, 'no more dramas/smeared mascara on my pillow'. While I was thinking about titles for the book, that song came to mind, as the title kind of summed up what I wanted to say.

I've written a lot of stuff over the years, with various great writers. A lot of it is yet unheard, which is a shame. I even wrote quite a lot of songs for a solo project, with the producers at Xenomania. However, that was right before I decided to take myself off to rehab, so I had to put my solo project on ice. Once I was out of rehab, I found it hard to move forward with my own projects. Let me put it another way: the way I was portrayed in the media, and the general perception of me, made it hard for me to move forward with it. I guess I'd come back wanting a fresh start, but wherever I turned I got the feeling that people were thinking, Ooh, hasn't she just come out of rehab? Perhaps we should steer well clear. Surely if someone puts themselves through recovery, it should be seen as a positive step rather than a negative one. It's someone who's asking for help and wants to move forward, rather than a person who is giving up and wallowing. There seemed to be a real stigma attached to the fact that I was fresh out of rehab. I felt a bit stuck, unable to move forward.

Unfortunately, once Hillary and I parted ways, I had a run of managers who weren't right for me at all and just seemed to see me as a meal ticket. While I was with Hills, I'd worked with some good writers, but some of the people who looked after me afterwards just wanted their percentage and didn't really help me in any way. I ended up doing some shitty jobs in shitty places. When I look back now, I realise that these weren't gigs that someone who'd achieved all the things that I had should be undertaking. The problem was, I was vulnerable. I felt like I had to be grateful and say yes to something, even when in my heart I knew I was worth more. I suppose I was trying to people-please. Maybe I thought that because I'd screwed up I had to take whatever was thrown at me. So I ended up working with a few people who didn't really know what they were doing.

After a few wrong moves, I put my faith in CAA (Creative Artists Agency). I knew they would look after me.

I have got to experience and appear on some pretty iconic TV shows in the last four or five years – some more successful than others.

My experience on *MasterChef* wasn't the best. It was the timing element that threw me. I'd always loved watching the show, and I love cooking, and I'm quite methodical about it. In my cupboards, I have a baking shelf, I've got a shelf for herbs and spices, and all my pots and pans are in specific places. I'm very anal about where everything goes in my kitchen.

I'm also a girl who likes to take her time when preparing a meal, sampling as I sip a glass of wine. Food seems to have become more like art on a plate these days, whereas I specialise in comfort food. For me, cooking is a leisurely pursuit, rather than a mad dash to finish, which is where I fell down on the show. The one thing I didn't have going for me was time. In fact, I ended up re-naming the show *ManicChef* because that's what it felt like. I just went blank during the tasks; I couldn't think what to do next.

When I did the Channel 4 skiing show, *The Jump*, I threw myself into it like a bull in a china shop. I'd been on a few skiing trips with friends in the past, and I guess you could say I'm a bit of an adrenaline junkie. I was certainly up for the challenge, that's for sure. Before the series started, I had a couple of assessments to

Over the years, I've been lucky to have been invited to some amazing events. And even luckier to have made special friends in the industry, including Peter Loraine (top left), Terry Ronald (bottom left) and ex-manager Hillary (below middle). But it was Mousey, who I first met on set of the 'Sound of the Underground' video, who would change my life by introducing me to Tommy (top middle).

My fans have always been brilliant, and have done so much for me. The Sarah Harding Addicts in particular have always been there for me in difficult times.

Pushing myself and my body on BBC show *Tumble*.

Coming from a pop background, I had no idea how hard the life of a touring musical theatre actor was. The whole process was a massive eye-opener.

When I did the skiing show, *The Jump*, I threw myself into it like a bull in a china shop.

Celebrity Big Brother: I'd gone into the house wanting people to see me for me. The funniest part about it was that I won. I won the damn thing! Maybe people had seen something else in me after all; I don't know.

Me in *St Trinian's 2*, my favourite of all the acting parts I did. During the filming, I was always being told I had to play it down and not get too excitable.

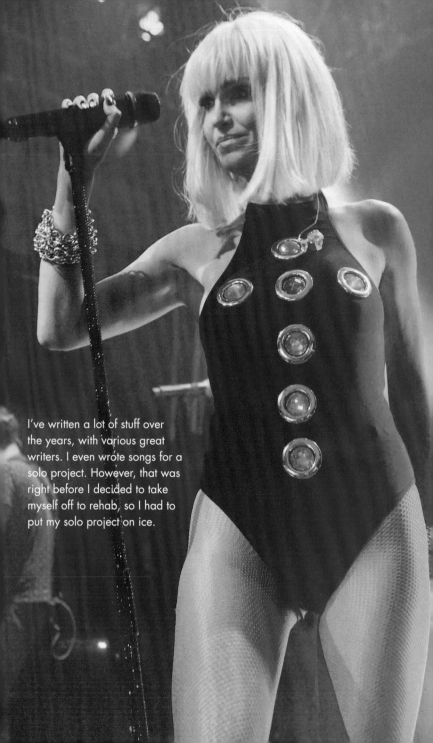

I've written a lot of stuff over the years, with various great writers. I even wrote songs for a solo project. However, that was right before I decided to take myself off to rehab, so I had to put my solo project on ice.

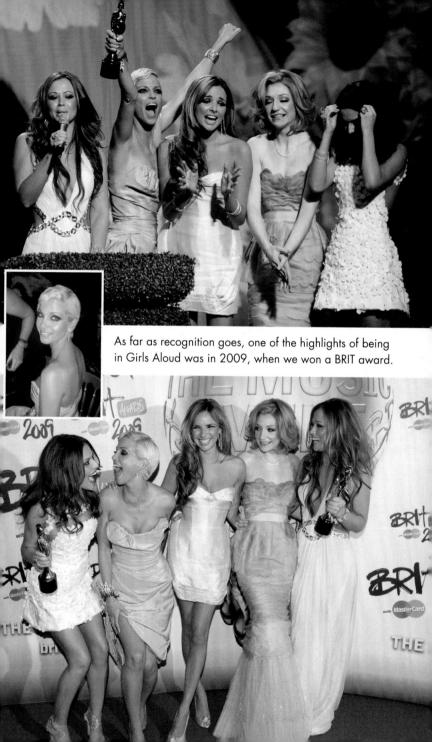

As far as recognition goes, one of the highlights of being in Girls Aloud was in 2009, when we won a BRIT award.

Music, friends and family have kept me going while undergoing treatment. Right now, I'm trying to find joy whenever and however I can.

see how well I fared, and I was just happy that I didn't fall over. Still, as the show goes on, there are all sorts of different techniques and elements to learn, none of which I'd done before. It was quite a tall order and not always easy.

My biggest accomplishment on the show was to beat James 'Arg' Argent on the snocross, where I fell over so many times. Towards the finish line, I fell down again and saw him coming up behind me. I remember thinking, there's no way I'm letting Arg from *The Only Way is Essex* beat me. So, I literally bum-shuffled across the finish line!

During the course of the show, I felt my knee go during jump training. Looking back, I should have been more cautious, but I so wanted to do the show. After seeing the physiotherapist, I decided to soldier on, despite the discomfort. When my knee went for the second time during training, I necked a couple of painkillers and got on with it. I'd done the medium-sized jumps, and I was determined to do the big jump. Unfortunately, it wasn't to be. By week five of the show, I had to pull out with a torn ligament. I ended up having major physiotherapy for about six months, completely out of action. But hey, I reached the semi-final, so it wasn't a complete loss.

It was tough because I couldn't work after being injured and it's not like there's much sick pay to be had when you're in the entertainment industry. I know I've been lucky, having worked all my adult life, but that's one of the things that's so upsetting to see during the Covid-19 pandemic, while the country has been in lockdown. While many people are on furlough, or claiming government subsidies, there are so many people who work in theatres and music who are struggling massively. The industry has almost completely shut down, with nothing open for months on end.

The TV show *Tumble*, in 2014, had been another physical challenge for me. This was a show where celebrities took part in gymnastics, with a judging panel of professional gymnasts and a weekly public vote. I appeared on the show alongside *Dynasty* actress Emma Samms, actor John Partridge and the lovely Ian 'H' Watkins from Steps, among others. The training was relentless and pretty gruelling, with eight hours training a day, but I thoroughly enjoyed it. It really appealed to my sense of adventure and my love of learning new skills, and, once again, I was keen to show people a different side to me. 'H' and I proudly ended up as joint runners-up, beaten by actor Bobby Lockwood.

I also nearly made the running for a big TV judging gig. In 2011, when Cheryl and Simon Cowell went to America to work on the US version of *The X Factor*, I was asked if I wanted to meet the show's producers with a view to becoming a judge on the UK version. I was on a skiing holiday in Val d'Isère in the French Alps at the time, staying in a big, beautiful chalet with Tommy and all his family. On the evening I got the call to fly back for the big meeting, we'd all been watching William and Kate's wedding on TV. This was the meeting that would help the producers decide between me and a couple of other contenders, including Tulisa and Mel B.

I arrived at Syco TV headquarters, which is in the Sony building, all ready to put my best foot forward, but there was a slight snag. I was brunette at the time, and I'd already been for a few meetings with the producers. Word had come back that Simon was a fan of my blonde-haired image, so Hillary asked our hairdresser to put a blonde wig on me for the meeting. During the discussions, they asked me all sorts of questions, including what I thought might improve the show, and what I thought might be my judging style and mentoring strengths. I wasn't convinced I had the right temperament for it, to be honest. I mean, I can barely sit still for five minutes, and I knew how long and gruelling those filming days and nights could be. Looking back, I wonder what would have come of it.

As everyone knows, Tulisa ended up getting the job, but it was nice to have been in the running. The funny thing is, I never really spoke to Cheryl about it because, for some reason, I felt a bit awkward about it, like I was after her job or something. Of course, that wasn't the case. She had chosen to leave the show, and they needed a new judge. I guess at that time we'd grown apart somewhat. It was during our three-year Girls Aloud hiatus, which was dragging on, and the distance between us seemed immense, I didn't feel like I could really talk to her like I had in the past. I'm so happy that isn't the case any more. I've always admired Cheryl because she's got gusto. She loves her fans, and she loves people, but she also can say 'no' when she needs to. She can be as charming as the day is long, but if she thinks something isn't right, she'll say so. I guess that's why Cheryl, along with Kimberley, were kind of the spokeswomen for the band. They're both very no-nonsense.

Cheryl has been so supportive during the past few months, and we talk a lot. In the early years of Girls Aloud we were very close, so it feels nice to have that back again.

Celebrity Big Brother was, for me, a disaster waiting to happen. When I try to think back about the reasons I agreed to do the show, I guess I thought it could be a good platform for me to maybe get back in the public eye in a positive way. Yes, I knew there were going to be a few tricky characters in the house with me – there always were on the show – but I felt like I had something to prove, not just to other people but to myself, too. I wanted to prove I could do it. I also went in there intending to show people a different side of me. I'd always been portrayed in the media as this mad, off-the-rails party girl. There may have been some truth to that in the past, but not at that point. It's not the sum of me and never has been. 'Hardcore Harding' is my caricature. She's a distorted exaggeration that I helped create as a way of fitting in, and of finding my place. Maybe this was a way for people to see a more complete picture. I mean, what's the worst that could happen? Famous last words!

I tend to wear my heart on my sleeve, and sometimes I forget myself and say too much. I like to think the best of people, and I try hard to please, but in doing that, I've sometimes tied myself in knots, and ended up fucking up, or making a bad situation worse. I think my need to people-please goes back to when my dad left home when I was 16. It was a tough time; my mum and I had moved up north, and I had to get to know a whole new set of people, right in the middle of my GCSE exams. When you're living with a group of strangers under close scrutiny, it's hard to be your true self or to please everyone. This is especially true when, all around you, people are trying to throw you off guard or wind you up. It is a competition, after all.

Having watched *Big Brother* and the celebrity version for years made the walk into that house seem completely surreal. I had such an incredible mix of feelings: fear, excitement, apprehension. I literately didn't know whether I was going to laugh or burst into tears, I was so overwhelmed. The one thing I do remember, as I made my grand entrance through the crowd towards the house, was the fear that I was going to end up being a puppet on a string. Dancing to somebody else's tune rather than my own. As it turned out, that's precisely what happened. I was easily manipulated. Unlike some of the other contestants, I didn't go into the house with a plan or much of an objective. When you look at the contestants in any *Celebrity Big Brother*, there are always some who are less well known than others, which sometimes means that the stakes are higher for them. They might have more to gain by being on TV every night for weeks on end. I certainly didn't go on the show looking for fame. I wanted to enjoy the experience. I wanted to have fun, be as open as I could and show people the *real* Sarah Harding. So, as always, I wore my heart on my sleeve.

In the end, this approach didn't do me any favours, and I'm not sure it changed anyone's perception of me either. Still, it certainly gave the show's producers the juicy TV they were looking for. I guess that's what *Big Brother* is all about. The format is tried and tested, and it works. What I learned was that however determined you are to not get swept up in all the bitchiness and mind-games, you still get sucked in. It's unavoidable. The house is a bubble; a society away from society. Once you're inside, you are so cut off from the outside world, that things that wouldn't usually be important are suddenly hugely exaggerated.

As was usual for the show, my housemates were a mixed bunch. They included Shaun Williamson from *EastEnders*, comedy actress Helen Lederer, *Hollyoaks* actor Paul Danan, *Most Haunted*'s Derek Acorah, singer and former finalist of *The X Factor* Amelia Lily, and Sandi Bogle from *Gogglebox*.

It all started off quite well in the house, and we were all quite friendly, but there was soon a very definite splitting off into different cliques – as there always is; that's when all the 'he said this, she said that' starts and animosity erupts. I had a particularly volatile time with glamour model Jemma Lucy, who never let an opportunity to fight with me go by. By the sixth day, I broke down in the diary room, telling Big Brother I couldn't cope with being in the environment as it was. I never really relaxed in the house, always feeling like a bird on a wire. I found myself watching the cameras to see if they were on me, feeling like I couldn't escape. Sometimes I even took off my microphone, just so I could feel like I was having a private moment. I couldn't even go to the loo without people listening, and there weren't any locks on the doors. FFS!

I don't know why I imagined that someone with my restless and changeable personality could cope with such an enclosed environment, especially given some of the hostility being thrown around.

It was like that movie, *The Truman Show*, and once you were in it, you couldn't get out – although I tried a few times. There were a couple of moments in the diary room where I lost the plot.

'I need to speak to my agent! I want to get out of here now!'

Every morning, at about 9.20am, I'd wake up, as if my body knew that the day was about to start and I needed to be on alert. Beyond the house were the walkways and corridors where the cameramen worked, and I could hear them walking up and down behind the big mirror in the bedroom. It made me feel on edge the whole time, like I was in a fishbowl. I clearly hadn't thought this through.

On the funnier side of things, I took in three massive suitcases full of clothes, but only had a tiny wardrobe to put them in. And so many pairs of sunglasses it was ridiculous. I'm the same every-where I go, never knowing what to take with me. This was over the top, even for me. I guess I just wanted to make a good impression.

My relationship with fellow housemate Chad Johnson was one of the big talking points of the show. I seriously had not gone into that place looking for love and romance. We got close because he was one of the few people I felt I could trust and confide in while I was in there and my only real ally. He wasn't a backstabber. The worst part about it was, I'd recently started dating a guy, who I knew must be seeing it all play out on TV every night. We had only been dating for a couple of weeks, and I didn't see it as serious at that point, but it wasn't a good look. In fact, when the other contestants weren't eating me alive, my guilt was. It was a mistake, and I messed up. After my brief relationship with Chad came to an end, post-*Big Brother*, we did get back together again for a while, but it was never the same. I don't think he ever forgave me, no matter how sorry I was. I pulled out all the stops to make it up to him, but he never really got over it.

I'd gone into the house wanting people to see me for me. I'd wanted to show people that I'm not just the crazy pop-star party girl who has problems with alcohol. I'm afraid I suffered at the hands of other people's jealousy and pettiness and then succumbed to my own demons.

The funniest and most surreal part about it was that I won. I won the damn thing! Just like in *Popstars: The Rivals*. Just when all the odds seemed to be against me, the public spoke, and I won. I just didn't get it. Maybe people had seen something else in me after all; I don't know.

It's funny, I was talking to Cheryl about my time in the *Big Brother* house just the other day, and she told me how much she enjoyed it. She thought it was absolutely hilarious! I must have done something right.

CHAPTER NINETEEN

CHERYL ON SARAH

The news of Sarah's illness hit me so hard. When Peter gathered Kimberley, Nicola and me together at my house to tell us – Nadine was away in Ireland – I went into shock. The worst part for me was the severity of the diagnosis. In the past, when I've known someone was ill, I've always felt able to say, 'Stay positive, you can get through this.' However, it was hard to find the positive in what I heard from Peter.

Since that day, she's been on my brain every waking hour – so much so that I feel like I want to be with her. Of course, that's not possible. There just seems to be so much up and down with what she's going through. Sometimes, she and I FaceTime, she sounds strong, and we can chat away happily for hours. Other times she's just wiped out. I suppose that's the nature of it; it seems so unpredictable.

Initially, I felt helpless. I struggled to find the right words to say when I spoke to her, and I didn't know what to do or how to be. I guess I'm one of the lucky people who've never really found myself in this position with a loved one before. In the end, I decided that I was going to call her, reminisce, and be as normal as possible. This was, after all, still Sarah – that same girl who's been in my life for almost twenty years now.

I think of myself as a spiritual person, and I guess Sarah does too, so there's been an honesty between us when we talk about what might be. I've always believed that the end of our life on Planet Earth isn't the end of everything and that we go to an incredible place once it's over. That's something I'll always keep reminding her. We've also made a pact that if and when she's left us, she's going to come back and visit me. We haven't decided exactly what form she might take, or what sign she might give to let me know it's her, but I said I don't mind as long as she doesn't come when I'm on the loo.

We both have this obsession with a TV show called *Ancient Aliens*. It's a documentary programme that discusses and presents possible evidence of extraterrestrial encounters throughout history. There are about fifteen seasons of it to date. You can call it conspiracy theories, but the guys on the show travel around the world studying old artefacts, historic sites and ancient writing, relating it back to the idea that alien encounters are documented in historical texts. Whatever your opinion, it's a fascinating theory and a great watch, and Sarah and I are both bang into it. We spend ages talking about stuff like that; it's a fun distraction for her, I suppose. Like most people, I've watched a lot of TV while we've been in lockdown, so I'll also tell Sarah any good TV finds I've made, and what she can binge-watch while she's resting between treatments.

Looking back, I think I had an instinct towards Sarah that was almost maternal, right from the off. Even though she's older than me, we always had that dynamic. She'll tell you herself how bad she was when it came to remembering choreography, and I remember being acutely aware of how stressed she'd be about it. Consequently, if she forgot her steps or her place while we were in the middle of a routine on stage, I'd literally leave my position to go and guide Sarah to hers. I still feel like that towards her now, only tenfold.

When Girls Aloud first came to be, I'd never met anyone like Sarah; she was the complete blistering blonde package. Ditzy and fantastically 'out there', she seemed outgoing and extroverted. To be honest, the rest of us were usually trying to put her back in her box, because she was such a wild child. She was also fiercely independent, and her moral compass was always on point. For instance, you all know how us girls like a bit of a gossip. While we were all gossiping about this person or that, Sarah was always the one to say, 'Oh, stop gossiping about people. Be nice!' That's probably the thing I love most about Sarah; she doesn't have a bad bone in her body. For all her wildness and craziness, there is not a malicious or nasty bone in her.

Sarah's downfall has always been her insecurity and not being able to recognise or accept all her great qualities. I've spent a lot of time over the years telling her how gorgeous she is; trying to get her to see the beauty in herself rather than the bad things. Sarah often concentrates on what she thinks are her flaws, but some of those flaws are the things I find beautiful in her. I guess that's what makes her such a confusing character. How the rest of us girls saw Sarah was not the way she saw herself. It was like two completely different worlds.

Sometimes, you might get more than you bargained for with Sarah. There were times when she'd come into rehearsals after a heavy night of partying and was just too tired to get through the day. Sometimes it was frustrating, but I'd try to see things from Sarah's angle. I'd ask myself why she felt the need to let loose so much; that there must be something behind it. I don't think I always had the answers, mind you. Sometimes, I noticed the tell-tale signs of when Sarah might be struggling. She might have broken up with a boyfriend but not told us about it yet, but I could tell it was coming because of the way she was behaving. There was a definite pattern.

The comedowns from all of that could be lethal and quite funny. There was one occasion when she turned up at Music Bank rehearsal studios – hoodie up, dark glasses on, Ugg boots. I knew straight away she wasn't feeling her best after a big night out. It got to the point that morning that she was so tired and frustrated with the rehearsal she threw a cup of tea across the room, missing Nicola by about a centimetre. There was tea up the wall and all over the floor. Looking back, it makes me smile. It's something we all laugh about now, even Nicola.

It was always my job to remove Sarah from those hyper situations. I'd sit down with her, talk to her and calm her down while she was going off on one. She was never mean or vindictive; she was just feeling the worse for wear and often more pissed off with herself than she was any of us. I remember having quite deep conversations with her at specific points. I tried to get her to tone down some of the things she was getting up to within that whole party scene. It was hard to be angry with her, though, because I always knew there was no malice behind what she was doing. I also knew that she was playing up to the image that she'd been handed; the one that she'd helped create. Through all of it, I knew a different Sarah. All of us girls did. The trouble was, it didn't matter how hard a person opened their arms to her, sometimes she just didn't know how to accept it.

For me, some of Sarah's best and funniest moments in Girls Aloud came on our final tour, Ten, after we'd all had a three-year break from one another. She was a real livewire on that tour, but not in a bad way. I guess she'd let go of the discipline of being in the band with four other girls, as we all had to a degree. That was when the mother-hen instinct in me really kicked in. I was forever reminding her where she was supposed to be on stage or letting her know when she'd missed her link to do or say something.

'Just keep an eye on me, and I'll give you a signal when it's your cue,' I'd say to her.

Of course, the moment she performed – when she was actually out there singing – she was always completely unique. Her voice would soar across the arena, and she'd deliver an incredible performance. She always did us proud and blew everyone away.

Now I just want to be there for her in any way I can. She might want to cry or rant or even have a laugh, but wherever it is, just be there. Mostly, I try to keep my own emotions in check, but on one FaceTime call with her the other day, I couldn't hold it in any more. She relayed some terrible news she'd had that day, and I lost it and started crying. I tried to move the phone out of the way so she couldn't see my face, but she knew what was happening. The mad thing is, it ended up with Sarah comforting me. 'Oh God, are you OK, babe?' she said through her tears. 'I wish I was there just to give you a hug.'

It was so, so heartbreaking. There was Sarah, going through what she was, and she was more worried about me.

To hear her talk about what might have been in her life, and what should have been, destroys me. It's broken me now, just thinking about it. A couple of weeks back, she sent me a song that she said summed up how she felt. It's by an American singer/song-writer called Beth Hart and the song is called 'Leave the Light On'. The lyrics talk about a woman who wants to live and love but has never really known how to. I listened to it at 8am in the morning and ended up sobbing. I don't want Sarah to have regrets, and I don't want her kicking herself for things she's done in the past. This illness would have happened to her regardless of how she chose to live her life. It is not, as some might suggest, a result of the person she is or has been. It's just one of those awful things that life deals a person sometimes. That's it.

When we all got together at Soho Farmhouse, there were no tears. Actually, that's not entirely true; there were tears, but they were from laughter rather than sadness. It was a lovely trip away for us all, and Sarah was at her best. She's always been funny and sharp-witted, but somehow, in all this, she's even funnier. God knows how! Maybe it's because she's more relaxed, I don't know.

I'm hoping to travel up to Manchester to see her before Christmas, and I'm looking forward to it. At the moment, I'm playing it by ear because I know how up and down she is with the new chemo pills she's on. Still, I've made her a personalised Christmas bauble to hang on her tree. Inside the bauble, there are shooting stars and a message that says, 'You have magic in you, Sarah!'

I want to hand-deliver my bauble so we can hang it on her tree together.

After that, we can get down to what's important – talking about aliens.

CHAPTER
TWENTY

've had a really shitty couple of days. The skin is cracking on my feet and all my joints hurt. I've been in agony, and it's been a struggle just getting around the apartment. If I'm sitting in one place for too long, or even when I wake up in the morning after a night in bed, I literally feel like I've seized up. My tendons and knees are killing me. I sometimes feel like I'm a hundred years old, and, apart from the soreness, the chemo tablets have made me really sick. I had to start retaking anti-sickness pills yesterday because it was so bad. The weird thing about this disease is that I just never know how I'm going to feel from one day to the next. It's like a bloody rollercoaster. Today, for instance, I feel OK. I woke up, felt good, so I had a coffee and got busy packing some stuff up to take to the apartment. My lawyer Tricia is coming tomorrow, and I always want to look my best when somebody comes, whatever the situation. The only thing is, I've got hardly anything to wear because almost all of my clothes are too small for me. As I mentioned, I've put on a lot of weight with the steroids, and let's face it, it's not like I've had much chance to go shopping.

Even when I am feeling well enough to go out to the shops, most of them haven't been open during the second lockdown.

Right now, I'm lying on the bed, having done my back in carrying speakers, which I'd brought from Mum's. We've been slogging away all day trying to pack and sort boxes, but I still don't feel like I've made much of a dent in it. It just seems endless.

The thing I'm trying hardest to deal with at the moment is the mastectomy, which I underwent a few weeks back. I wasn't ready to talk about it then, and I'm still not sure I am, but here goes. It was something that I'd hoped wouldn't have to happen, but looking back, I suppose it was inevitable. I remember the surgeons saying that they would make a drawing of what parts of my breast needed to be taken away, and it was virtually all of it. They also took a skin graft from my back, somehow managing to work around my tattoos.

Coming round from that operation was one of the worst moments of my life. I'm so grateful that Mum was there waiting for me because when I woke up I just screamed the place down.

Now there's just a bunch of stitches where my breast used to be. As much as I know it had to happen and I want to be brave, I can't look at myself in the mirror any more. There's something wrong with the image, and I can't face it. On top of everything else, I just don't look like me any more. I don't recognise myself. It's very hard to wake up every morning knowing that a part of me is missing; that part of my womanhood is gone. The loss of it breaks my heart. Some women can have reconstruction, but I know I'd just end up back in intensive care because I'm too ill. I suppose it had crossed my mind at one point, the idea of reconstruction, but now I have to be realistic. I have to let go.

Sometimes, it's like every single part of your body is screaming at you that you're not the person you think you are in your head; that you can't possibly be that person again. That's how I'm feeling right now. I want to get back to normal so badly. It's all I want, just to feel like me. But I know that's never going to happen again.

I was only ever meant to do the first half of the *Ghost – The Musical* tour. The idea was that if it was mutually agreed and it went well, I would potentially do the second half. Unfortunately, it did not go well, but the stories that came out in the press about my time in *Ghost* were inaccurate to say the least.

I'll admit that there were good shows and bad shows during my run playing Molly Jensen, but to say I was thrown in at the deep end was an understatement. The truth is, coming from a pop background, I had no idea how hard the life of a touring musical theatre actor was. I certainly didn't factor in the toll singing eight shows a week would have on my voice. The worst part, however, was that nobody prepared me for it. The whole process was a massive eye-opener for me – getting used to terms like upstage right, downstage left. Then there were lighting cues and spots to hit, and, of course, a script to memorise and deliver. It might have all been a bit easier had we not had just three weeks of rehearsal.

As soon as rehearsals started, I got 'the fear' big time, but despite expressing concerns to my management of the time, everyone just seemed to think it would all be fine. The show's producers were happy to have me on board, of course, because they felt I was a name that would sell the show. I don't think anyone really thought much past that.

By opening night, some members of the ensemble didn't seem particularly happy about me being there. In fact, it could get quite bitchy at times. Having the lead role in a musical theatre production when you don't come from that world seemed to put a few of the actors' noses out of joint. I told myself it was the fact that they'd trained hard and worked for years at their craft that made it hard for them to accept me, but it hurt nonetheless. People would be charming to my face, but then I'd hear that the same people had a different opinion of me when talking out of my earshot. Then there were the looks and the eye-rolling when I messed up, which I'll admit I sometimes did.

The run was exhausting. We'd play one theatre for a week, and after the Saturday night show, we'd load out and travel to the next venue under our own steam. After the show, I'd always have a big crowd of people waiting outside the backstage area who wanted photos and autographs. There was no way I wasn't going to spend time with my fans. I was quite often the last one out of the theatre with the long drive ahead of me. By the end of each week, my voice had pretty much gone. There were times when I'd end up crying once I'd come off stage because I'd lost my voice. There was one particular show in Dublin where I left the stage feeling devastated. My voice just wasn't trained for that kind of singing, so sometimes I didn't have the vocal stamina. What upset me most was the idea that I couldn't sing, which was what I was hearing from some quarters. I think I proved during ten years of being in Girls Aloud that I could certainly do that at least!

Another problem was the knee injury I'd sustained doing *The Jump*. I had a ruptured ACL (anterior cruciate ligament), and I was still having physiotherapy when I got the part in *Ghost*. I was also taking some prescribed painkillers. These pills were necessary and certainly helped with the pain, but they weren't always the best thing for my mental sharpness, as I found to my cost.

Despite all this, there were good times during my run in *Ghost*. I made three good friends during the run: Jacqui Dubois, who played Oda Mae, and is a renowned actress and singer – and doesn't take shit from anyone! Andy Moss, who played Molly's murdered lover, Sam, and Tarisha Rommick, who played Louise. They were lovely and supportive, and would sometimes warn me who to watch out for – the gossipers and the eye-rollers who'd been all sweetness and light to my face. Whenever it was just the four of us, it was great fun. We'd go out to a Wetherspoons for a gin and tonic after the show, and I felt like I could let my hair down and be myself.

As well as arranging our own transport, we also had to organise our own accommodation, so in Blackpool, Tarisha, Jacqui and I decided to rent a place together. It was sold as a penthouse flat but was actually more like something out of *Fawlty Towers*. As we all breezed through the door, expecting something a little bit smart, we were horribly disappointed. The brown swirly seventies-style carpet was one thing, but discovering we had to feed the meter with pound coins to keep the gas and electric running was a real shocker. Looking back on it, I can laugh. It was Tarisha's birthday while we were there, and we made the most of it, celebrating with wine and cupcakes from Tesco.

It was in Blackpool, however, where 'the incident' happened, which is where some of the more colourful media stories about my time in *Ghost* came from.

We were halfway through a show when I was informed by one of the stage managers that I wouldn't be going back on for Act Two because he thought I seemed unsteady and unfocused.

'You're not in a fit state,' he said. 'You couldn't do the potter's wheel scene properly, and with the lights and everything else, it's just not safe.'

I'd been struggling, for sure. The raked stage, with me singing and dancing in heels, wasn't great, and then there were about nine floors to run up if I needed to zhuzh up my make-up between scenes. And there was a lot of zhuzhing on that show, with lots of crying throughout. Believe me, some of those tears were real.

I don't understand why they waited till halfway through to pull me off. Why did they even let me go on in the first place if they were worried? Press reports said that I was slurring, unsteady on my feet and possibly drunk. I wasn't drunk, and I wish I'd had someone on my side to stand up and defend me, but that was the story everyone got.

Maybe I'm oversensitive and sometimes take things too much to heart. Still, if I feel a terrible atmosphere or energy around me, it makes me really anxious. Now, I felt like everybody was waiting for me to fuck up; waiting for my next mistake. There were times when I could actually see it coming from the wings: the eye-rolling and laughing. It was an awful situation, which doubled my stress and made me even more anxious. The thing about live theatre is, unlike other things I'd done in the past – filming or recording in a studio – there's no second chance if you go wrong. If you fuck up, it's there for all to see. Little mistakes can sometimes be covered up, but big ones can't.

At the end of my contract, I knew I wasn't going back for the second half of the run. I didn't want to, and I knew the producers didn't want me to either. Andy was also only signed up for the first half but ended up going back. He's a hard worker, and I really admire him for it, but at the end of the day, I was the only member of the cast not to go back. There were people from the backstage team that only did part of the tour, but I was the only actor. I suppose that was the reason people assumed I'd been sacked from the production. That wasn't the case. It was utter bollocks, in fact. I finished my contract and the shows I was contracted to do.

When I look back on it now, I feel like I was blindsided. Maybe I was naive about how hard performing for eight shows a week in a musical would be for me. The truth was, my management wanted me to do it because they thought it would be good for me, and for them, and the producers wanted me to do it because I could bring in the punters. Everybody thought I should do it, but perhaps nobody truly considered whether I could.

Some of the songs in *Ghost* were tough for me because they involved vocal mixing, which is not something that came naturally to me. The mix voice is when a singer combines chest and head voice together. You have to sort of thin your chest voice out so it can switch from low notes to high notes without anyone really noticing the transition. I hadn't been trained to do that. I could sing in a strong head voice when needed, but my natural vocal style was a powerful chest voice. I mean, give me something by Bonnie Tyler, and I'm well away. Some of these songs, on the other hand, left me struggling. In the second act, there was a song called 'Rain', which had a bit more gusto. In that part of the show, my character, Molly, has found out that her husband Sam's murder wasn't a random act, and that the psychic who's been helping her with the case might be a fraud. There's now anger in Molly, and this is a powerful belt of a song. I enjoyed singing it, but even then I got into hot water with the musical director. He didn't like the rasp in my voice and told me to try to smooth it out.

'That huskiness is my natural voice,' I told him. 'Plus, I've been singing eight shows a week; my voice is tired, which only adds to the rasp.'

He kept telling me off, though, and at one point I was so pissed off I walked out of a soundcheck. Everyone knew the kind of voice I had when I was hired. In the short rehearsal period, I'd had no training or relearning to sing for musical theatre. To be honest, I think it was a case of, she's a name, let's get her in, sell some tickets and worry about it later.

It's funny: one of my fans secretly recorded me singing the big song in *Ghost*, 'With You', during one of the performances. When they sent it to me, I was happily surprised. I think I just had it in my mind that it had all been such a disaster, but it was actually a really lovely recording, and I sounded so much better than I'd remembered.

Maybe if I'd had more time to prepare, it could have been an entirely different experience.

CHAPTER
TWENTY-ONE

Ever since I was a little girl, I wanted to be a singer or actress. I wanted to be on the stage and to entertain, but I never really thought about everything that goes along with it. I'm a sensitive person when it comes down to it, and I take everything to heart. I'm a big believer in spiritualists, healers, crystal healers and the like. I know it's not for everyone, but I've tried many of these things that I believe have helped me on my journey. Most of them have told me, in one way or another, that I'm prone to taking on and absorbing other people's feelings and making them my own. It's why I don't deal well with negativity.

When I was in the band, I could always sense if one of the girls was in a bad mood, or something was about to kick off. My intense dislike of confrontation was such that I would feel extremely uncomfortable and agitated in those kinds of situations. It was probably because I knew that once I lost it, I really lost it. I could go from 0 to 100 in ten seconds, as if a red mist had descended. It was best not to be around bad feeling and conflict, and my constant wariness of it – being on high alert the whole time – was often exhausting. I was always trying to sort my head and body out. Nobody could accuse me of not trying to help myself, that's for sure. I once did a strict detox in a clinic in Austria with my friend Steve, where you had colonics, lymphatic drainage, liver wraps and the like. It was supposed to clear out our systems, but we were always starving. Within a few days of being there, all the toxins and crap were seeping out of my body – but I looked bloody awful. We ended up cycling for miles in an attempt to find something sweet to eat, finding sanctuary in a doughnut shop, where, realising we were from the clinic, they took pity on us.

One of my other excursions, to a meditation retreat, also wasn't the oasis of calm I expected it to be.

It all came about because I was supposed to have been going abroad to do charity work, but nobody informed me that I needed certain vaccines to be able to go. The vaccines couldn't be organised in time to be effective, so the whole thing fell through. It wasn't the first time that I'd had to pull out of a charity trip. In 2009, a team of famous faces, led by Take That's Gary Barlow, were the first to trek up Mount Kilimanjaro for Comic Relief. Also on the trip were my bandmates Cheryl and Kimberley, plus Fearne Cotton, Alesha Dixon, Ronan Keating, and Denise Van Outen, among others.

Initially, I'd been supposed to undertake the trek with them. In fact, I was one of the first to sign up. As the thought of it sank in, however, I started to think that I'd made a rash decision. I'd always had this underlying back and spine problem, and I was worried about how gruelling the trek was going to be. The last thing I wanted was to be moaning and complaining all the way up a mountain, getting on everyone's nerves. Eventually, the Comic

Relief team were pushing for a final answer. Although they said all the right things to encourage me, I decided not to go. I was scared that my body couldn't take it. It's one of my biggest regrets, I think. Apart from the whole adventure of it, it was amazing how everyone bonded on the trip. That's something I would have loved to have been a part of and one of the reasons I'd so wanted to do the charity overseas.

Once the second charity trip was definitely off, Mousey told me that she'd heard about this three-day meditation retreat, which sounded blissful. The experience offered reiki healers, meditation gurus, sound-baths and shaman. It was all very New Age and peaceful and also private – just what I needed. The fact that two places on the retreat came up, just as we found out I wasn't able to go on my charity trip, was clearly a sign.

From what we'd been told about the retreat, it involved lots of work around love, especially self-love, and I thought it would be a good thing for me. Often, the biggest problems I've had in life have been rooted in feelings of rejection and my abandonment issues. Maybe this was something that might help me heal in some way. The scariest prospect was the rules about what you could and couldn't do in the week before the retreat commenced: no drinking; no red meat; no bedroom activities! I think they just wanted you to have a clear head before you started, and I actually did all right, managing all of that. Well, apart from one bedroom activity with my boyfriend on the night before it began, which I don't think did any real harm.

The event was held in this long, converted barn, which had kitchen facilities at one end, and several set-ups outside the barn for different healers, reiki masters, psychics and the like. Upstairs there was an office, which was where all the event's organisers, staff and helpers based themselves.

The initial and central part of the retreat involved a ceremony around eating the root of some white plant. I guess it was a bit like ayahuasca, which is a sacred shamanic plant medicine from the Amazon. It's said to have intense cleansing and healing properties, as well as a slightly hallucinogenic effect. What we had was something similar, although, unlike ayahuasca, it wasn't illegal in the UK. The idea of it is to help you find your inner spirit, your inner child, or maybe, as I did, your spirit animal. Mine was a Cheshire cat, with a scary grin, which flickered like an old movie, coming closer and closer to me with every blink.

During the ceremony, everyone wears little white robes, and you're all on the floor with furry rugs. It's seen as a very sacred ceremony, and for someone of the right mindset, I'm sure it is wonderfully healing.

On my first night there, the shaman decided that the headache I was experiencing was a hex on my brain, so he placed his hands on my head to remove it. Then it was time for the ceremony, which was to last all night. I remember wondering why there were bowls all around the room where the ceremony took place, and that question was answered during the first few hours. The thing about ingesting this plant root is, it makes you purge. It's meant to take away any badness and negativity inside you. Your enteric nervous system is known as the 'second brain' or the brain in the gut, and the root helps you purge anything bad lurking in there –

sadness, trauma or whatever. It's meant to be healing. This means that once you've taken it, you're actually throwing up – all night! Now, as I've explained, I am not good with people throwing up around me. In my younger days, I was practically phobic about it, and it's certainly not something I want to do in front of other people. So as you can imagine, once this thing took hold, I was absolutely mortified, rolling around in the corner, doing my absolute damnedest not to be sick.

'I don't wanna be sick, I don't wanna be sick,' I kept saying, while the shaman kept a close eye on me. I was literally doing everything in my power not to vomit.

Not long into the evening, the pain in my head returned – the hex. Not surprising really, as while all this was going on, people were going around the room shaking rattlesnake percussion instruments and banging blocks and bongos in your ear. I did try. I tried my best to feel the music, to let it go through me, to see visions and to heal myself. My overriding thought, however, was that I was going to kill Mousey for not telling me what I was in for with this ceremony. She knew I hated anything to do with sickness and knew damn well I wouldn't have come if I'd known what was involved.

While all this was going on, Mousey was in the upstairs office, where participants could talk to helpers, get a drink or go to the loo. Concerned about my general wellbeing, the shaman went up to speak to the helpers.

'There's someone downstairs who is not in a good way,' he said diplomatically. 'She's not in a good way at all.'

'Is it my friend?' Mousey said, but the shaman didn't want to say out loud.

Meanwhile, Mousey was thinking, please, God! Please don't let it be Sarah!

The shaman and his wife, who was a healer, told Mousey, 'If it does turn out to be your friend who is unwell, don't engage or have contact with her. Don't even look at her. She has to go through this and deal with it on her own.'

I think by then Mousey knew that I was the subject of the conversation. The next thing she knew, I'm being ushered upstairs into the toilets, crying and feeling hideous. In the end, I gave in and let myself be sick, and I immediately felt better. It had been the feeling that I was going to vomit and my aversion to it that had made me feel so terrible.

By the time I came out, Mousey was there, waiting for me.

'I'm going to fucking kill you for this,' I said.

On the second day, I felt a bit better, but I was just so drained. The bloody 'hex' was back again with a vengeance, and while the experience was nowhere near as bad as the previous night, I still felt like I needed help.

'Go outside and find the thousand-year-old tree,' the shaman said. 'That will help you!'

Mousey and I walked outside, then wandered around, searching around for the sanctuary of the thousand-year-old tree. We were both in our little white nighties – although I'd now teamed mine with black Ray-Bans in an attempt to halt my banging headache.

'Is that it?' I said, pointing into the distance.

'No, that's not it,' Mousey said. 'I think it's this one.'

When we got to the tree, we lay down beneath it, but within seconds I burst into tears. Thinking I was laughing, Mousey started giggling, loudly.

'What are you doing?' I said through sobs. 'Why are you laughing at me?'

'I thought *you* were laughing,' she said. 'I'm sorry.'

'I'm not laughing, this is hysterical crying,' I said.

'But why?' she asked. 'Why are you crying?'

'Because this is not the right tree,' I said.

At that point, the shaman appeared.

'What are you girls doing? That is the wrong tree. That's not the thousand-year-old tree. It is over there.'

He pointed to the tree that I'd initially pointed out to Mousey.

'I KNEW IT!' I shouted.

This was all her fault, but looking back I find it very funny.

By that point, it was impossible not to see the ridiculousness of the situation. There I was, Sarah Harding from the glamorous pop group Girls Aloud, lying in my nightie at the supposedly healing tree with Ray-Bans on, like Patsy Stone from *Ab Fab* – at the wrong bloody tree.

Mousey didn't have the heart to tell me at the time, but when I got up, I had twigs, cobwebs and a spider in my hair. Meanwhile the shaman stood, pointing and shouting at us, while we tried not to laugh.

'This is really fucked up,' I said.

253

As the retreat continued, I did my best to do what I'd gone there for and dig deep into my inner psyche. There was lots of meditation, considering thoughts and feelings, getting them out and writing them down. I have to say, after the disaster of that first night, I began to get into the swing of it. In the end, the retreat brought out a lot of positivity in me; more than I'd ever felt before. Yes, I was absolutely shattered when I finally got home, but the lasting effects of what I'd been through were quite remarkable. One of the things it taught me was that you had to learn to endure and get past the rough to appreciate the smooth. It taught me to continually remind myself of my objectives and goals. I'm hoping maybe that's something I can put into practice with what I'm going through now.

CHAPTER
TWENTY-TWO

After selling my house in Buckinghamshire, I'd been renting a place, which turned out to have some sort of lurking infestation. All of a sudden, I noticed that I was getting bitten here, there and everywhere, and I couldn't work out why. Once I realised that the place was infested, I started to stress out to the point where I wasn't getting any sleep. At one point, we got pest control out to bug-bomb the place, but nothing seemed to work. I ended up staying with friends and in bed and breakfast accommodation – anything to get me away from that house. Eventually, I had to get rid of or destroy so much of my furniture, because it just wasn't fit for purpose any more.

One night, I stayed up late, working on some music. For me, it wasn't just the composition that took time, it was getting to grips with how to use the technology needed to record and mix it. I'd often start in the evening and end up working right through to the early hours. I'd be completely engrossed and lose all track of time, but I didn't mind. I always loved hearing the results. With all the turmoil of everything else around me, music was something to focus on and kept me sane.

Anyway, this one late night, I was sitting on the floor, playing my guitar, when I started to realise that one of these bites had turned quite nasty. The area in question, my left lower-thigh, was excruciating and felt almost as if something was trying to burrow its way inside me. This eventually led to a cyst that went septic, and, because it was there for so long, started making me very ill. My temperature rocketed, and I felt horrendously sick. Before long, I was in and out of sleep with a fever. My mum took my temperature, which turned out to be much higher than it should be, so she managed to get a doctor to come out to us.

On examining me, the doctor said instantly, 'She needs an ambulance now!'

Before I knew it, I was in the hospital, dangerously ill, being treated for sepsis. It was a horrendous time, but the doctor had managed to catch it and halt it before any significant damage was done.

On the day I was about to leave the hospital to go home, I felt something painful under my arm while I was washing. My first thought was that it was something similar to what I already had, caused by a bite, but there was something different about this. As I felt around, I realised that my lymph nodes were enlarged, and it felt tender.

I mentioned it to the doctors, who told me that I'd need to go to a separate clinic because that wasn't their field of expertise. I told them that I would sort something out.

It was December 2019, and I'd just starting seeing a new boyfriend. I felt a bit better, so I kind of forgot about the lumps under my arms and carried on. At one point, the lad I was seeing pointed out how big my boobs were getting, but I still didn't think anything of it. My boob size had fluctuated before. When I was with Girls Aloud, performing on the Tangled Up tour from May to August of 2008, they seemed to disappear completely. This was mainly because of all the dancing I'd done during gruelling rehearsals and on tour.

In the end, I went for an ultrasound, but the news at the end of it wasn't exactly consoling.

'I think this might be something that needs to be looked at more closely,' the doctor told me.

I was advised to schedule an MRI, but before that happened, the world changed in what seemed like an instant. Coronavirus hit – the dreaded Covid-19 – and everything either went into slow motion or stopped altogether. On top of that, I had to move out of my rented house the day before the whole country shut down.

Now we were in lockdown, and by now I was living at my mum's. I was aware that I needed to get this health issue sorted, but with everything that was going on, it was tough. At the start of the pandemic, there was so much conflicting information about hospital appointments, with the main message being to stay away unless it was a real emergency. What kept me calm, was my firm belief that this was just a cyst. I'd been playing my guitar a lot, and I thought the strap had probably irritated the area around my breast. I just had to stay brave. There hadn't been any cases of breast cancer in my family. Plus, after what had happened the previous year with the infected bite, I probably just assumed it was more of the same. The trouble was, the pain was getting worse. It got so bad while I was living at Mum's that I couldn't sleep in a bed any more. I slept on Mum's sofa, popping painkillers like they were smarties. I really overdid it, but the pain was overwhelming. Eventually, my skin started to bruise, and by now I was terrified. I'd been waiting it out through lockdown, but Covid wasn't showing any signs of going away, and it was just getting worse and worse. I could see blisters forming, and that was scary.

One day I woke up realising that I'd been in denial about the whole thing. Yes, there was a lockdown, yes, there was a pandemic, but it was almost as if I'd been using that as an excuse not to face up to the fact that something was very wrong.

Feeling sicker and sicker one day, I called and spoke to someone at the hospital. A woman asked me exactly how many painkillers I'd taken, and when I told her, she told me I needed to go to A&E as soon as possible. I knew she was right, but that didn't stop me feeling scared at the prospect of walking into a hospital. I wasn't exactly thinking straight, and all any of us had seen on the news was how terrible the situation in hospitals was during the Covid pandemic. I just didn't know what to expect.

My fear wasn't exactly eased when I got there either. Everyone I came into contact with was in full PPE gear, and suddenly everything I'd seen on the news was right there in my face. As scared as I felt, though, it dawned on me just how amazing these people working at the hospital were. They were as calm as anything, putting their lives on the line to help people, simply doing their jobs, while I was in the midst of a panic attack.

I was put on antibiotics, and I explained the issues with my breast to the doctors, which was why I'd taken so many painkillers. The doctors told me that I needed to get my breast looked at properly as soon as possible.

With lockdown easing slightly, it was time to act. I finally went back down south, on my own, for an appointment where I had an MRI. This time, I was able to see a highly recommended doctor, who a friend knew and had put me in touch with.

I went alone because of the hospital rules around Covid. After that, there was another appointment, this time for a biopsy. I'd always been close to Tommy's sister, Anna, who really was like a sister-in-law to me, and still is. She offered to come with me, and she was brilliant. So supportive the whole way through. I'm just so grateful she was there for me.

All through the tests, I was, of course, praying that it wasn't cancer. I think the fact that what I had was so painful gave me some hope it might not be. I'd read and been told that cancer lumps are often not painful, which is why I was hoping against hope that what I had was just a cyst of some kind.

Anna also came to the appointment where I got my results. The worst of all days.

When we got there, there were three medical professionals in the room, which Anna later admitted to me she immediately took as a bad sign. Let's face it: if there was nothing sinister to report, why would it take three people to deliver the news? A doctor, a surgeon and a breast nurse, all were looking solemn. When I looked over at Anna, I could see the worry on her face. This was not good.

When the doctor delivered the news that I had breast cancer, I was a mess – like anyone would be. Being faced with your own mortality is not something you consider, but that's how that moment felt for me. I just remember thinking: well, that's it, game over. The oncology breast nurse tried her best to make me feel better.

'Sarah, there are so many things that can be done these days,' she told me. 'You mustn't give up hope.'

Whatever else she said to me barely sank in. My head was spinning. How was I going to process this news? How was I going to get by from day-to-day with the knowledge that I was suddenly fighting for my life?

CHAPTER
TWENTY-THREE

Anna's initial thought was that I should go straight into hospital. She rang around the hospitals, but said I should stay at her place that night, so we could work out the best way forward. The first thing I did when we got there was open a bottle of wine. I know it probably wasn't the best idea, but it was my go-to in times of acute stress. Anna was very understanding.

'I'm not convinced you should be drinking, babe, but I'm not going to have a go at you,' she said. 'You've certainly got good cause, and you probably need it right now, so you just do whatever you fucking need to, to get through the next few hours.'

That evening, we got through a couple of bottles of wine together. Eventually, I passed out, and Anna put a pillow under my head and tucked me in under a duvet. The following day, after Anna had delivered the news to my mum, it was suggested I go to Watford General Hospital in Hertfordshire. I guess they could see what kind of a state I was in when I arrived, so I was put in a side room on my own, rather than on the ward.

The thing I learned very quickly was what amazing human beings nurses are. I always knew how hard people in the medical profession worked, especially in the NHS. Still, having these people around me 24/7 was a real eye-opener for me. They're angels, doing the job that they do, especially for the comparatively small amount of money they get. No one should ever underestimate how hard they work. Those nurses sat with me at night as I cried, and it was in those moments when I realised that what they were doing was more than just a job. They were caring for me, as they do all their patients. Actually, genuinely caring, even at the end of ridiculously long shifts.

As time went on, I found myself getting to know some of them, and I'd often ask, 'What time did you start today?' I'd always be surprised to hear that they'd started very early in the morning, and yet here we were, late in the evening. In the end, I started taking it on myself to brighten their days if I possibly could. Whenever I was having a relatively good day, I tried a bit of a laugh and a joke with them; a little bit of banter to keep them smiling.

Some of them would ask me about life in Girls Aloud, and I'd tell them stories about our antics on tour. I recall telling one nurse about the time I was so hungover on stage at one of our gigs, that I was convinced I was going to throw up. The nurse giggled as I told her how, when I had to get from the A stage to the B stage in a vast arena, I didn't think I was going to make it without being sick. With only a Perspex walkway under our feet as we travelled from one performance spot to the other, I was thinking, Oh my God, I'm going to throw up. I'm going to throw up over the audience, everyone is going to see me, and we'll all be traumatised for life. It's not as if we were in a blackout during the transition, and with giant screens behind us the whole thing would be beamed out to the audience in full HD. When I got to the B stage, I could see our manager Hillary looking up at me with a face like thunder: angry but worried. I could see her willing me not to throw up. That was the kind of story I kept the nurses entertained with whenever I was feeling up to it, hoping to brighten their day a little bit.

While I was at Watford General, I requested a medical detox because I wanted to know that I had a nice clean body before I started any treatment. I'd been drinking a bit because it had helped to numb the pain. Although it hadn't been anything over the top, I still wanted to make sure all that was out of my system before they started to pump me with anything else. When a person's body becomes dependent on something, whether it's prescribed or otherwise, sudden removal can cause physical and psychological symptoms. Detox provides a safer environment for withdrawal from drugs, alcohol or whatever under medical supervision. For this, I stayed in a regular ward rather than in the side room.

'I've got curtains around the bed,' I told the nurse. 'I can just keep them pulled around if I want privacy.'

The only problem with that was some of the other patients were struggling to cope with dementia. On any hospital ward, there's always a real mix of patients, and some are doing worse than others. I had one particularly scary night when a guy from the other end of the ward was wandering around threatening to beat people up. On another occasion, a woman spent the night yelling at everyone to get out of her house. To be honest, the way I was feeling during the detox, I'm surprised it wasn't me running up and down the ward, shouting.

The way I got through it was to keep the curtains pulled around my bed, put my headphones on and watch *Friday Night Dinner* on my laptop. I felt vulnerable and scared about what was happening to me, so I thought it best just to keep myself to myself. The nurses even decided to use my middle name, Nicole, to help keep my privacy.

I started off on some antibiotics, painkillers and Diazepam to help me sleep, as well as some morphine for the pain. I wasn't going to have my cancer treatment at Watford General, so that was about as far as it went.

It was such a weird time, where I was trying to process what was happening to me, and I remember crying a lot. There were some really nice ladies in the beds next to me. Whenever they could hear that I was upset, one of them would call out, 'Are you all right, Nicole?' which was the name above my bed. They'd watched me going backwards and forwards for X-rays and CT scans and all the rest of it; I guess they knew I was in a bit of trouble.

When I arrived at The Christie Hospital in Manchester, that's where the work really began. There were more X-rays, more CT scans, more MRIs. The doctors there were so thorough, trying to find out what they were dealing with and exactly what the spread and the damage might be. I learned more about my body and what was going on with it than I ever thought I'd need to, and that has continued throughout.

One of the first things I had to have was a port fitted in my chest, where the chemotherapy drugs could be administered. Plus several other smaller ports for drips and other things. It was like being bionic, and needles were coming at me from every angle. Like many people, I bloody hate needles, although I've kind of got used to them now. When you have cancer, needles are all part and parcel of it – whether it's injections, blood taking, lines to administer drugs, or saline drips and flushes. It's non-stop needles.

Once my port was fitted, everything seemed hunky-dory at first, but after a couple of days, I felt like something wasn't as it should be. The area around the port felt sore and swollen. When the doctors checked it out, they agreed it didn't look normal, but the fact that the swelling felt like it was going into my neck was even more of a concern. I don't really remember much after that. I only know what I've been told. At some point after that, my blood pressure fell dangerously low, and I was rushed into intensive care. I had sepsis, which, as you probably know, is the body's extreme response to infection, causing a chain reaction in your system. It's considered a medical emergency and most undoubtedly life-threatening.

Straight away, my port was removed, but with both my lungs and my kidneys failing, doctors decided to put me into a medically induced coma. The only way I was going to survive was to be in a deep state of unconsciousness, with ventilation to keep me breathing. Even then, the doctor wasn't sure he was going to be able to pull me back from it, so advised Mum to prepare for the worst. While I was out, I had lumbar punctures, where a needle was inserted between my vertebrae to remove a sample of brain and spine fluid. I also had more brain scans, which revealed that I also had a condition called posterior reversible encephalopathy syndrome, also known as PRES. It's a pretty rare condition, and it's when parts of the brain, usually at the back, are affected by swelling.

While I was under, the nurses asked my mum what kind of music I liked to listen to and what shows I liked on TV, so they could have stuff on in the background. They felt like it would be good to give me something familiar to take in.

'She loves *The Big Bang Theory*, *Family Guy* and *Friday Night Dinner*,' Mum told them, so that's what got played in the room while I was in my deep slumber, as well as some of my favourite artists – Pink and Lady Gaga.

I wasn't in that room, however. I was in another world. I remember having the most horrible dreams during it all, but I could never put my finger on precisely what happened in them. Just that they were awful. Situations I couldn't get out of, no matter how hard I tried. I have recollections of being on some sort of quest, but not being able to find or obtain the thing I most needed. I remember everything being larger than life and otherworldly, as if I was in a movie like *Labyrinth* or *The NeverEnding Story*. If ever there was a twilight zone, this was it. There was no warmth, no comfort, just fear and a need to escape.

I do remember opening my eyes at one point, but not being able to speak. I looked up at Mum, tearful and rubbing my arm as she talked to me.

'We all love you, Sarah. I miss you, the dogs are missing you. Love you.'

I wasn't sure if I was dreaming then, but I think now I'd just woken up for a moment. God knows what Mum must have been feeling, knowing I might not come back.

I was in the induced coma for almost two weeks, but when I was first brought out of it, I didn't wake up. That was a worry for a while. I eventually came round and stayed in intensive care for a further two weeks. During the time I was in the coma, I had no idea about all the things that were happening to me or any of the treatment I was given. Even once I was off the ventilator, I still couldn't speak properly. All I could do was make these noises that sounded like a chimpanzee trying to communicate.

I hadn't been awake more than half an hour before I wanted to get up and out of bed, but Mum told me off.

'You've always been like this,' she said. 'You've always wanted to just get up and go, especially when you're not allowed.'

That went on for a while. In my head, I was a normal, fit person, all ready to walk away from it all. As far as I was concerned, it was: 'Thank you very much for all you've done. I'll be off now and back next week for chemo.'

At one point, I really did try to get up, and the nurses freaked out, gently pushing me back down on the bed. There were so many lines, a catheter, wires and God knows what coming out of me. What on earth was I thinking?

'If you get up off that bed now, it'll cause a bloodbath if you rip all these lines you've got in you,' one of the nurses said.

It didn't matter anyway. No matter how much my brain was telling me I needed to move, my body simply wouldn't comply. It was like being a prisoner, stuck inside myself.

Even when I did eventually try to get up, with help, my legs wouldn't carry me because of muscle wastage. It was such a weird feeling, not feeling supported, and I'm still struggling with it now.

Of course, when I couldn't get my own way and go home, I wasn't best pleased. At one point, one of my close friends spoke to Mum, and the conversation went something like this.

'How is she doing, Marié?'

'Well, she told me to fuck off the other day, so …'

'Right, so she's getting back to normal then.'

I was probably on so many drugs when I said it, I'm sure I wouldn't have meant it. Poor Mum!

During the fortnight I was in ICU it was the nights that I found the hardest. Such was the severity of it all that I had to have a nurse with me 24 hours a day, to keep an eye on me. I found myself stressing and worrying about all the things that might have happened to me while I was in the coma. Two weeks of my life, gone. I had thoughts and what felt like memories. None of them were very nice, but I couldn't work out whether they were flash-backs or dreams – all the scans I'd had, the lumbar punctures, the drips going in and out of me as I slept. The thought that I wasn't present in the world for all that time scared me. My comfort was those fantastic nurses, who'd kept notes of what was going on every day so they could fill me in now I was awake.

Worse still was the fear I had of sleep. Once I was out of the coma, I forced myself to stay awake for as long as I could, refus-ing to close my eyes, terrified that if I shut them again, I'd go back under and not wake up. This went on for three days, and one of the nurses, Jude, stayed awake with me for two of them. On the third night, another nurse took over. When Jude came in for her shift later that night, she came in and sat on the other side of the bed.

'OK, now we'll all go to sleep together,' she said.

That night, I finally gave in and agreed to take a sleeping pill. The two nurses put their heads down on either side of my bed, and we all went off to sleep together.

Once I was out of intensive care, I was adamant that I wanted to leave the hospital and recover at home. In the end, the doctor sat me down for a serious talking-to.

'Look, Sarah, you can barely walk. If you go home now, you'll be back here in two days for sure. Only this time you'll probably be even worse.'

It was frustrating. I felt like I'd been in hospital for so long by that point. I just wanted to be out in the fresh air, to look at something ordinary, some real life.

That said, I think I surprised the doctors at how quickly I recovered after coming out of ICU. I had help walking and getting out of bed, plus physiotherapy to show me techniques for movement and gaining back some of my lost muscle mass.

Everyone seemed happy to see me back on the ward. I wanted to be happy and get back to being the comedian there, which had sort of been my default setting while I was there before. I wasn't quite there yet, though. I think I was in a state of shock at what had happened to me, which isn't all that surprising really. Everyone understood; they knew it was going to take me a few days to get back to my old self. There were some nights when I'd lie in bed, looking at the space around me, and I'd cry. I was in such despair. I would ask the nurses, 'How did this happen to me? Why is this happening to me?'

They would just hold me and cuddle me and let me cry. Simply being there for me in a moment where I felt utterly lost.

They'd also stay with me if I had bad dreams or woke up in agony. They'd sit with me until I settled, and chat to me about all sorts of things to take my mind off what was happening. It's quite unbelievable what these nurses go through for and with their patients. They can be comforting somebody who's dying one minute and dealing with someone who is angry and wants to fight with them the next. We owed them all so much already. After 2020 and the pandemic, we owe them everything.

CHAPTER
TWENTY-FOUR

'm not going to lie, I was crapping my pants before my first dose of chemotherapy. I'd heard people talk about it, and I knew people that had gone through it, but I just didn't know what to expect or what was going to happen once all that stuff was inside my body. The whole idea of it made me extremely nervous and sick. I just wanted it over with. When I realised it was just a drip, I felt better. What I also didn't realise was that any side effects weren't going to happen straight away unless I had some kind of instant allergic reaction to it. Any nasty bits would be further down the line, once the toxic but essential medicine started to do a number on the disease.

While I was in the hospital with plenty of time to kill, I even started to make a little video diary. I figured if I could get through this, maybe talking about it later could help other people who found themselves in the same position. I thought documenting how I felt at the time might be a good memory-jog down the line. Anyway, here's a snippet of where my head was at that time.

I had my chemo yesterday. It wasn't as bad as I thought, but now I'm just waiting on the after-effects. All I know is that I'm feeling exhausted today. I had a cold cap on during my chemo to try to save my hair. That's not necessarily going to work. I do know that I'm going to lose my eyebrows and eyelashes, so who knows if I'm going to hold on to my lovely blonde hair? Actually, there's not much blonde left anyway. Thanks to the global pandemic, I'm going down with roots!

I've had a really shit night. I can't sleep through. It's 5.30am, and I've woken up almost every hour through the night. It's not surprising, really. Today I had more scans and more blood tests to find out if my cancer has spread. It's a waiting game now, I suppose. I'm trying to keep positive, but that's not something you can brush away, is it? And then there's the pain; there's been a lot of that.

I know I must look awful because I don't even feel like myself any more. It's the steroids I've been taking, they make me look bloated. So much so that I asked the nurse to cover up the mirror in my room because I can't bear to look at it any more. It feels like something is trying to take over my body, and we're in a race to try to stop it. The grim reality is, I've had to come face-to-face with my own mortality. It's quite the pivotal moment, that realisation of all the things you've taken for granted, and of how fragile life can be. Also, the thoughts of how different things might have been. How I might have done things differently.

On top of all that, I'm worried about my living situation. At the moment, I'm at my mum's, complaining like a petulant teenager. I can't stay there forever. I need to sort out somewhere to live up north because I need to be close to my mum now. There's no way I can get through this without her by my side. The problem is, many of my friends are down south so I feel cut off. Still, I suppose we've all been cut off this year, haven't we?

In fact, after that first treatment, I really didn't feel anything at all. I just felt like the same person in the same body. I have pictures of that first chemo, and with that cold cap on I looked like I was about to blast off – rocket man!

At first, the chemo didn't affect me in the way it does some people. Although from what I can gather different people can have varying experiences, depending on the type of chemo they're having and how their body reacts. For me, sickness wasn't so much of a problem. My issue has been the awful pain in my joints, particularly my knees when I'm trying to get around. In fact, getting up and down stairs can be an absolute nightmare. The other thing that's been tough is the steroids. They are supposed to help build you up while you're undergoing treatment, but they're also very bloating. The toll they've taken on my weight is one of the hardest things I've had to deal with. I've always been reasonably slim; in fact, during Girls Aloud, when I was literally dancing my arse off, I was a proper 'skinny bird'! These days, I hardly recognise myself, but steroids are just one of those things I have to endure; they're a vital part of the treatment.

The other thing about steroids is that they can make you extraordinarily chatty and hyper. I know what you're thinking – she's hyper at the best of times, so what the hell is she like on steroids? At one point, it got so bad that a psychiatrist at the hospital suggested it might be a good idea to keep me in for my own wellbeing, but as it turned out, he was way off the mark.

On the day I was due to leave the hospital to go home, I'd been booked in to chat to a psychiatrist after my chemo session.

They wanted to check on me, just to see how I was coping with what had been a traumatic, life-changing event. That day, I'd had an extra dose of steroids in my meds, post-chemo, so by the time I got to see the psych, I was jabbering away, nineteen to the dozen. I mean, can you imagine that vast surge of chemical energy on top of my ADHD? I was on the ceiling, to be honest, so, so happy about the prospect of going home, full of energy and non-stop talking. The other thing was, I had an incredibly dry mouth because of the chemo, so getting the words out as fast as they were coming was quite challenging. This, I'm sure, made me sound even more strange, and there was a certain amount of dribbling going on too. At one point, I noticed the psych and his sidekick peering at me, suspiciously.

'Sarah, have you taken anything today other than your meds?'

'What do you mean?' I asked. 'I've had half an eggcup of medication, and I've got a bloody dry mouth. Of course I haven't taken anything except what I've been given.'

'You haven't taken anything else?' he said.

'No, I'm just excited to leave,' I said, turning to the other guy in the room. 'Can you tell him, please? It's just the medication that's making me all weird.'

'I just want to make sure you're in the right place, Sarah,' the psychiatrist said.

That was when the other one chipped in. 'How do you feel about staying in the hospital a little bit longer, in another part?'

That was when the penny dropped; they wanted to put me into the psychiatric ward. They didn't believe I wasn't on something other than what I'd been given. I guess that's a measure of how much the steroids were affecting me.

'Look, I haven't taken anything illicit, I just want to go home,' I said. 'What the fuck's wrong with that? Seriously!'

Looking back, I know they were just trying to look after me, but at the time I was angry, not to mention scared.

'There's nothing wrong with me other than the steroids,' I said. 'I'm going home.'

And guess what – I went home. By that time, I'd been in hospital for almost eight weeks.

When I got back to Mum's, I did my best to get my head together. The one thing I was clear on was that I didn't want my cancer diagnosis getting out into the public domain.

'I don't want people to know,' I said to my mum. 'I can't deal with all that attention on me, and having people ask questions.'

I didn't even want all my friends and family to know. At first, I kept it down to Anna and my mum, my lawyer Tricia, and Mousey – that was about it. At that time, I didn't even tell Fran, who has since been a little pot of gold, helping to look after me through all of this.

People noticed the difference in me, and I could feel it. The effects of the steroids were obviously quite pronounced in me, so there was a couple of times when even my mum asked me if I'd 'taken something' while I'd been on them. I suppose because I've been in rehab a few times for one thing or another, people who are close to me are often on high alert. When they see such a dramatic change in me, it can cause them to freak out.

I guess the steroids have a similar effect to, say, cocaine in the way that they make a person over-chatty and hyper. I can't really comment on other drugs, because I don't have experience with them. I never liked smoking weed, and as for anything else, well, I was always too scared to take anything that lasted more than twenty minutes.

So far, I haven't lost my hair with the chemo, and that's because I use the cold cap each time I undergo chemotherapy. For those of you who don't know, a cold cap is a hat you can wear during some types of chemotherapy treatment. The cooling effect of it reduces blood flow to the scalp, which also reduces the amount of chemo medication that reaches the head. I put it on about fifteen or twenty minutes before my treatment starts, and I have to say, it's not the most comfortable feeling in the world. It does what it says on the tin, so it's freezing, and it can give me a headache. With experience, I've found that if you can get past the first ten minutes, your head goes completely numb and then you're OK. Even worse than that, for me, are the cold mittens and slippers that go with the cap, which help to prevent neuropathy – nerve damage in the hands and feet. I can hardly stand the hand mittens – that's the cold that really goes through me.

For a while, it seemed like the chemo was working. The lumps went down, and the blisters started to fade. I'd been hopeful until I began to notice it all coming back again. I remember thinking, something's not right here.

As my treatment progressed, I was adamant that I didn't want the news about my diagnosis getting out. However, there was a little part of me that thought, maybe if I could bring myself to talk about it, it might help some other people who are going through something similar. There had been so much reporting on the news about people missing out on check-ups during Covid lockdown, even though they might be worried about something. People who had left a cancer diagnosis until it might be too late. Maybe if I spoke out, as a public figure, a celebrity, it could help get the message across how important it is to get checked out if you have concerns. That's something I plan on doing if I can.

As scary as it was to go public about my diagnosis, it was the right thing to do, and the amount of support I've received since is incredible. I've been inundated with lovely messages from my fans, and I couldn't love them any more than I do. I'm grateful beyond words for that.

CHAPTER
TWENTY-FIVE

Unlike a lot of people in the entertainment industry, I'm relatively low-key when it comes to social media. In fact, I'd barely been on it for the two years before my diagnosis. Although I did miss chatting with my fans, I felt like it could be a bit of a minefield sometimes. I was always scared of saying the wrong thing and then being trolled by loads of haters. People who don't happen to agree with me or haven't got anything better to do than to make nasty comments from behind the safety of a computer keypad. Even with an announcement about my cancer diagnosis, I was worried about saying the wrong thing and getting involved in some political row or having to read random people's opinions about me. Especially if I didn't like what they had to say.

At the start of 2020, Peter Loraine texted me, just to say hi and see how I was doing. After that, we'd just started chatting again from time to time – catching up on WhatsApp about our dogs and various other things. A few months later, once I'd got my cancer diagnosis, he was still messaging, but by then I was finding it hard to get back to people. I just didn't know what to say to anyone. In the end, Peter sent me a text asking if I was OK, as he was a little bit worried that he hadn't heard from me. I looked at the message and thought about it for a moment. Peter was always somebody I felt I could trust. Perhaps he might be able to help me find a way to deal with any unwanted media attention if someone got wind of what was happening.

I texted Peter back: *If I tell you something very personal, can you promise not to tell anyone else? If so, I might need your help.*

Peter promised to keep my secret, so I texted to say that I'd been diagnosed with breast cancer. He was shocked and upset, of course, but when we spoke on the phone, he was calm and understanding.

'The reason I asked if I can trust you is that I don't want anyone to know,' I told him. 'I can't deal with the press and other people's opinions. For now, I just want to keep it close.'

Later, on a Zoom call, I explained to Peter in more depth.

'Right now, the only people who know are you, Mum, Mousey and Anna – that's it, I said. 'I can't tell anyone else because there are so few people I trust.'

I guess that was a sad thing to admit, but after the way things had been for the past couple of years, it was the truth. The funny thing is, after I finally went public about my diagnosis, a few people have come out of the woodwork who I haven't seen or spoken to for ages. Acquaintances who have my number but haven't contacted me for years, suddenly messaging me: 'Are you all right, babe?' or 'Devastated to hear your news'. It feels like they've seen something that they think is a big news story and message me purely because they have my number in their phone. 'Have you heard about Sarah Harding?' they say to their friends. 'It's so sad. I've just sent her a personal message.' There's a difference between those people and the people I can call real friends – the ones who've stuck with me through everything. As I said earlier, I can count my real friends on one hand.

Peter said that I could totally trust him not to tell anyone. He said he would help me as much as he could, and, as I had no management or representation at the time, he would steer the ship if and when the time came to make an announcement.

A while into my treatment, someone alerted me to a tweet that somebody had put out. It said, *'Does anybody know why Sarah Harding is at The Christie Hospital?'*

I'm not going to lie, I completely freaked out when I saw it. I think I'd built up the idea of nobody finding out about my illness so much that this sudden chink in the armour set off major alarm bells in me. Surely now people were going to start asking questions. The press would start digging.

I called Peter, who agreed that it might not be long before the tweet started circulating among fans and people started asking questions.

Not long after that, someone at the hospital sent me a tweet saying that she had sat by my bedside one night. It was a public tweet rather than a private message, so now the cat was really out of the bag.

This meant it was probably time to 'go public'. Peter suggested we should do this via my social media platforms, which he said he would help me reactivate. This would be preferable to an exclusive press interview, which he thought could look cheap and open me up to all kinds of unwanted drama with the media. If I made my own short statement through my own social media, the announcement would be on my terms, rather than it having the spin of a journalist. I trusted him, so agreed to follow his advice.

Before the announcement, I would have to tell my family, friends and loved ones. There was no way I wanted people I hadn't yet told to find out through a news bulletin, or through rumours on the internet. While I geared up for that, Peter contacted Twitter and Instagram to get all my login details – which I'd long forgotten, having not used them for two years. After that, he made a little schedule for the week, indicating how it would all unfold. With news like this, we knew we had to be prepared. Part of that schedule would be to let my Girls Aloud bandmates know. I asked Peter if he could arrange to meet the other girls from the band and tell them personally. Meanwhile, Mum and I could tell anyone that I felt needed to know. This included other people in my family and people who were close to us.

Nadine was in Ireland, so he told her over the phone, but he met all the other girls at Cheryl's house, and delivered the news to them together.

Once that was done, on Wednesday, 26 August, at 10am, I took to Instagram and Twitter for the first time in two years to share my news.

Hi everyone, I hope you are all keeping well during these uncertain times. I've not posted on here for so long, thank you to everyone who has reached out to check in on me, it really does mean a lot.

I feel right now is the right time to share what's been going on. There's no easy way to say this, and it doesn't feel real even writing it, but here goes.

Earlier this year, I was diagnosed with breast cancer and a couple of weeks ago I received the devastating news that the cancer has advanced to other parts of my body. I'm currently undergoing weekly chemotherapy sessions, and I am fighting as hard as I possibly can.

I understand this might be shocking to read on social media, and that really isn't my intention. But last week it was mentioned online that I had been seen in hospital, so I feel now is the time to let people know what's going on, and this is the best way I can think of to do so. My amazing mum, family and close friends are helping me through this, and I want to say a thank you to the wonderful NHS doctors and nurses who have been and continue to be heroes.

I'm doing my very best to keep positive and will keep you updated here with how I'm getting on. In the meantime, I hope you'll all understand and respect my request for privacy during this difficult time. Sending you all so much love … xx.

It was so essential for me to explain things in my words and not have the story leaked or reported incorrectly. I didn't feel like I had a lot of control over my life at that point in time; this announcement was at least one thing I could do on my own terms. We knew that the press would call for further clarification, so we added contact details for Peter's management company and Simon Jones PR. Simon is a close friend of Peter's and also Cheryl and Nadine's publicist. Now, when the press enquired, we could tell them that at this time, what I'd written in the post was all there was to say on the matter.

Sure enough, within six minutes of the post going live, the story was on every news site and every radio and TV news bulletin. It was out. In fact, Kirsty, one of the Fascination team, told Peter she stepped off the train at Euston at 10.30am, and it was all over the LED news screens around the station. In the week that followed, Peter told me that 100,000 new people followed my Instagram account. Isn't it strange how that kind of news affects people?

I was in turmoil at home that week. There seemed to be so much going on. Apart from the terrible worry of the illness itself, I was upset and freaking out about what everyone else was saying. Meanwhile, the *Daily Mail* ran with a headline: 'Britain's most glamorous hell-raiser: How Girls Aloud's "Hardcore Harding" became famous for wild partying, explosive love affairs and stints in rehab, but now faces a battle against cancer'.

It was full of stories of me being a wild party girl, of me falling out of clubs, of me being a 'caner'. They illustrated the piece with the now-famous photo of me drinking from a bottle of whiskey. It was a horrible story. Even the messages on the *Daily Mail* message board commented on how the piece was below the belt. Everyone else was kinder with their stories. In my statement, I'd asked the press to respect my privacy because I was terrified there would be photographers camped outside Mum's house or following me to and from the hospital on my treatment days. Mum had enough on her plate without fending off journalists on her doorstep. In fairness, the press has so far respected my wishes and I'm grateful for that.

What was really lovely was the messages of support I received either via social media or through people contacting Peter's management company, Fascination Management. Not just from friends and followers, but from others in the entertainment industry, some of whom I didn't know that well, but who had taken the time to reach out with kind thoughts. Knowing how I must be feeling after the announcement, Peter collected them into an email and sent them over to me. I was quite overwhelmed. Among many others, there were messages from Fearne Cotton, Perez Hilton, Duncan James, Sadie Frost, Fifi Geldof, Keith Lemon, Katie Price, Ella Henderson, Keisha Buchanan from The Sugababes, Shayne Ward, Susanna Reid, All Saints and Rylan Clark-Neal. I was very moved, reading them all.

In those first weeks, my diagnosis, and the thought of all the treatment that was to follow, just felt like the highest and most terrifying mountain to climb. It was comforting to know that people were not just thinking about me and reaching out, but also spurring me on to beat this thing.

CHAPTER
TWENTY-SIX

Hearing from all the girls again really lifted my spirits. I was so happy when Peter suggested organising a couple of days away so that all of us could be together. I guess you could call it a Girls Aloud reunion.

The plan was for us to go to Soho Farmhouse, which is a private members club and hotel on 100 acres of farmland near the Cotswolds – part of the Soho House Group. We knew it would be low-key and private there, and besides that, it was only two hours from my mum's house, where I'd been living during my cancer treatment. A trip to London would have been too far, and it didn't seem like a good idea for me to be that far away from the hospital and my doctors.

On the one hand, I was really looking forward to hanging out with the girls again. Apart from anything else, having cancer and going through treatment often feels like you're living on another planet, separated from the rest of the population. Everyone else around you seems to be going about their business: going to work; going out to dinner; hanging out with friends etc. Meanwhile, a person going through chemo has an entirely different experience of the world. It's like you're living in this weird bubble. So, when I was feeling up to it, any opportunity to get out into the world had to be grabbed.

I did have my reservations and fears about the reunion get-together, though. It was going to be the first time we'd all seen one another in about eight years. That in itself was nerve-wracking enough, but the fact that I felt and looked the way I did made it worse. Going through cancer is bad enough, but the side effects of all the stuff that's supposed to make you better can sometimes be as difficult to deal with as the disease itself. The steroids I'd been taking made me look bloated, and I'd lost my eyelashes due to the chemo. As the time for the reunion drew closer, I was picturing them all turning up looking fabulous and glamorous, while I looked … well, like I did. Not myself. Not my best. It's not that I thought they wouldn't understand or be judgemental, of course; it's just that when we were together as a group, part of our thing was the glamour. As a band, we all had our own styles and looks, but there was a sexiness and glamorousness about Girls Aloud that I just wasn't able to rise to then.

Still, I wasn't going to let that stop me, so a few days before the trip I went shopping to get some new outfits. A friend of mine has a boutique near Mum's place, and she was happy to help me out, finding some new gear.

On the day, I arrived at Soho Farmhouse just as Nicola, Nadine and Kimberley pulled up, so actually, the reunion moment was mainly in the car park.

We all stayed in the same big house, and we had the most amazing Japanese dinner delivered in from Pen Yen, which is one of the beautiful restaurants within the farm.

By then, I'd loosened up and started to enjoy myself. There was much reminiscing. We decided to watch all the episodes of *Girls Aloud: Off the Record*, which was the documentary-style behind-the-scenes TV show we'd made for E4 in 2006. The show followed us in the run-up to our Chemistry tour that year, along with the filming of the 'Whole Lotta History' video in Paris. Around that time, we were also doing promotion in Australia and New Zealand, Ibiza and Greece. All this stuff was included in the episode, which, looking back with hindsight, seemed hilarious. We were all so different then; there was a sort of sweet naivety about us. I remember Cheryl in particular almost watching her old self through fingers over her eyes, mortified at some of her comments and antics. There was a difference in how the girls were then to the sophisticated women they'd since become. I'm not so sure about me. I think I've continuously remained brash and lairy. Maybe that's something to be proud of.

Nadine was particularly funny during the watching of the show.

'I've never seen this,' she said. 'I don't remember doing any of this.'

Peter reminded us that none of us wanted to do the show in the first place and that he was the one who'd persuaded us all to do it. The rest of us had all agreed eventually. Nadine had been the only one who stuck to her guns and said no, but in the end was outnumbered. Maybe that's why she didn't remember doing it – perhaps she'd erased it from her memory.

Watching *Off the Record* provoked lots of laughing and even more cringing, but I have to say, I looked on fondly.

'You only miss this when it's gone,' I told the girls.

My classic scene was where I crashed a Ferrari. Peter got a call at the record label asking, 'Are we insured for this?'

CHAPTER TWENTY-SEVEN

Over the years, Girls Aloud worked with many charities and, given my situation, it's something that I would like to continue with if I can. Mainly for Macmillan's or The Christie Charitable Fund, which provides enhanced services for The Christie Hospital, over and above what's provided by the NHS. The Christie is one of the largest cancer treatment centres of its kind, and the hospital where I've received the majority of my treatment. What I'd really love is to put on some sort of charity gala or big fundraising event by way of a massive thank you. It's something I've talked to Cheryl about, and, having done so much for The Prince's Trust, it's something she feels she might be able to help me with.

It would undoubtedly be something positive to look forward to and to get dressed up for. Just find me a good stylist and a make-up artist, and I'll be there. Let's face it, I still have to look good standing next to those other four girls, if they come and join me.

Even if I'm not around to see an event through, I need to let the people there know how grateful I am to them for all they've done for me.

It's strange, I keep thinking about funerals at the moment. It might sound morbid, but it's hard not to at this stage: cemeteries, plots, burials, what kind of send-off I'd like and how it would all go. It's all there front and centre in my mind. I've also thought about an epitaph for my grave. I'm thinking 'FFS' might be a good one. It's probably been my most used phrase throughout this, with one crappy event following another. 'For fuck's sake!'

In a couple of days, we have a meeting at the hospital to discuss the possibility of an alternative chemo treatment. In truth, I don't even know if there is one. What I do know is that if the one I'm on now is the only one they have, then I'm in trouble. I just can't cope with the underlying effects of it, and I don't want to any more. Feeling as I do is not how I want to live out whatever time I have left. If this is going to be it, then I would prefer to stop chemotherapy altogether. Instead, I'd take some CBD to help me manage the pain, and leave it at that. I know at some point I will have to make a call on what I want my quality of life to be, and if the doctors can't do much more for me, then I'd rather come off the chemo and move on. I know now that the disease has progressed further and is running through me. However, I don't know where I am with the original breast cancer site at the moment, as I'm post-radiotherapy and awaiting another test.

Still, the tumours on my lung have gotten more prominent, and then, of course, there are the brain lesions. They are what worry me the most at the moment. I think they are what's causing me to feel dizzy and confused sometimes. I feel like a 90-year-old a lot of the time. I'm not steady on my feet, and if I start having dizzy spells and seizures, who knows what will happen? I really don't want to be put into an induced coma again, that's for sure. When it comes down to it, I'm just not living my life how I should be, and at some point soon, I'll have to make a decision about how I might change and take control of that.

On 17 November 2020, my 39th birthday, I went to The Christie for my chemo, but when I got there, my treatment room wasn't ready.

'Can you just hang out in the coffee room, Sarah?' the nurses said. 'We just need to change the sheets on the bed; it won't take long.'

When I eventually walked into the room, there were cupcakes, bags of presents and cards. The nurses had laid on a little birthday surprise for me. I can hardly put into words what this small, simple gesture meant to me. I'd always tried to be nice to the nurses, to crack a joke and make them laugh while they were looking after me. I guess I must have done something right to receive such kindness from them that day. It was quite overwhelming.

Right now, I'm trying to find joy whenever and however I can. It might be roasting a chicken or watching *The Queen's Gambit* on Netflix. It's definitely spending quality time with Mum and seeing my friends whenever I can. True, life has got so much smaller, and my priorities have changed, but the other Sarah Harding is still in there somewhere too, trust me. Given half a chance, I know she'd be back with a vengeance, dancing on tables and laughing and joking with everyone. Making people smile is one of the things I'm missing most because it's what makes *me* smile.

I think what I'd really like to do is to see everyone – all my friends, all together. One last time. Then I'd throw a great big fuck-off party as a way to say thank you and goodbye.

Wouldn't that be amazing?

JANUARY 11TH 2021

At the start of 2021, we've all found ourselves in another national lockdown. It's not the best start to a new year, but this time, thankfully, there are now vaccines available. While that gives us all a bit of hope, we all know it's going to take a while before everything gets back to normal, especially as far as health services go. I know there are going to be women, just like me, who find themselves lost in the pandemic, and perhaps not getting checked out when they feel like there's something not right. Worrying about getting appointments or visiting hospitals, or simply pushing other health issues to one side. All I can say is, please, girls – please, *everyone* – don't let anything get in your way – get checked out if you're worried about something. Of course, I can't know for sure, but I believe that if I'd got things moving with appointments and check-ups faster than I did, I'd probably be in a better place than I am now. I think I would have had more options for treatment, and certainly less spread of disease. It's a bloody hard pill to swallow, but the best I can hope for is that my experience might encourage other people to get themselves sorted as soon as possible.

Before I finally put this book to bed, I wanted to share a little bit of positive news. MRI scans at the end of December revealed that the tumours in my brain and in my lung have shrunk a bit with the treatment. I don't know exactly what that means for me, but at least I know it's moving in the right direction, and right now, every little victory feels momentous. With this news under my belt, I was able to enjoy a relaxing quiet Christmas with Mum, and yes, I got plenty of lovely Christmas pressies. At the moment, I'm just grateful to wake up every day and live my best life, because now I know just how precious it is.

ACKNOWLEDGEMENTS

To my best friends Anna, Fran, Jodie, Mel and Mousey, I couldn't have survived this last year without your ongoing love and support. Thank you all a million times over – I love you.

With special thanks to Sara Cywinski, Tricia Grout, Peter Loraine, Terry Ronald and Simon Jones.